U.S. Dept. of Agriculture

Record of Experiments

conducted by the commissioner of agriculture in the manufacture of sugar

from sorghum and sugar canes at Fort Scott, Kansas, Rio Grande, New

Jersey, and Lawrence, Louisiana. 1887-1888

U.S. Dept. of Agriculture

Record of Experiments

conducted by the commissioner of agriculture in the manufacture of sugar from sorghum and sugar canes at Fort Scott, Kansas, Rio Grande, New Jersey, and Lawrence, Louisiana. 1887-1888

ISBN/EAN: 9783337272302

Printed in Europe, USA, Canada, Australia, Japan

Cover: Foto ©Andreas Hilbeck / pixelio.de

More available books at **www.hansebooks.com**

U. S. DEPARTMENT OF AGRICULTURE.

DIVISION OF CHEMISTRY.

BULLETIN   No. 17.

RECORD OF EXPERIMENTS

CONDUCTED BY THE

COMMISSIONER OF AGRICULTURE

IN THE

MANUFACTURE OF SUGAR

FROM

SORGHUM AND SUGAR CANES

AT

FORT SCOTT, KANSAS, RIO GRANDE, NEW JERSEY, AND LAWRENCE, LOUISIANA.

1887–1888.

WASHINGTON:
GOVERNMENT PRINTING OFFICE,
1888.

15449—No. 17

INTRODUCTORY LETTER.

UNITED STATES DEPARTMENT OF AGRICULTURE,
Washington, D. C., January 26, 1888.

SIR: Complying with your instructions I beg to submit herewith for your approval Bulletin No. 17 of the Division of Chemistry, containing a record of the experiments made by your direction in the manufacture of sugar from sorghum and sugar canes.

The bulletin is divided into three parts, viz:

PART I, *experiments with sorghum at Fort Scott.*—Containing the report of M. Swenson; drawings and description of apparatus; a digest of the report of E. B. Cowgill to the State board of agriculture at Topeka, Kans.; and a statement of the action taken by the Department in respect of certain letters patent granted to M. Swenson for the use of lime carbonates in the cells of the battery.

PART II, *experiments at Rio Grande.*—Containing the report of H. A. Hughes, drawings and description of apparatus used, and analytical notes.

PART III, *experiments in Louisiana.*—Containing the report of H. W. Wiley of the results of the experiments conducted at Lawrence, La.

In obedience to your further orders, I took charge of the chemical work of the three stations. During the summer of 1887 the necessary apparatus and chemicals were purchased and sent to the several stations. Of my assistants, C. A. Crampton and N. J. Fake were directed to take charge of the analytical work at Fort Scott, and were furnished with written instructions for their guidance in taking samples and the general method of analyses to be followed.

F. V. Broadbent and H. Edson were sent to Rio Grande. They had the same instructions as were given my assistants at Fort Scott. In addition to this I personally directed the beginning of their work. On October 14, 1887, Mr. Broadbent resigned his position in the Department for the purpose of pursuing his studies abroad. Mr. Edson from that date had sole charge of the analytical work until the end of the season.

On April 2, 1887, G. L. Spencer was sent to Fort Scott to secure the removal of certain machinery to Lawrence and joined Mr. Barthelemy in the work of preparation at that station.

At the close of the work at Fort Scott, Dr. Crampton and Mr. Fake also came to Lawrence to assist in the chemical work at that place.

3

In the following pages only such chemical data are given as are necessary to illustrate the experiments made. Much of the chemical work is yet undone, and it would delay too long the publishing of this bulletin to wait for its completion. All the details of the chemical work for all three stations will therefore be collected and published in a separate bulletin, viz, No. 18. The success of the work at all three stations has been most gratifying, and the diffusion process for the manufacture of sugar has been advanced beyond the experimental stage by the labors of this Department, beginning in 1883, and it is now offered to the sugar-growers of the country with the confident assurance that it is the best, most simple, and most economical method of extracting sugar both from sorghum and sugar canes.

Respectfully,

H. W. WILEY,
Chemist.

Hon. NORMAN J. COLMAN,
Commissioner.

PART I.

EXPERIMENTS WITH SORGHUM AT FORT SCOTT.

LETTER OF TRANSMITTAL.

FORT SCOTT, KANS., *November* 9, 1887.

SIR: I herewith submit my report of the experiments in the manufacture of sugar from sorghum cane, conducted at Fort Scott, Kans., during the present year.

I beg to acknowledge my appreciation of the hearty support that you have accorded me while in charge of this work.

Very respectfully,

MAGNUS SWENSON.

Hon. NORMAN J. COLMAN,
Commissioner of Agriculture, Washington, D. C.

REPORT OF M. SWENSON.

Previous to my appointment to take charge of the experiments in the manufacture of sugar from sorghum cane at Fort Scott, Kans., all attempts to make sugar from this source in paying quantities had failed. This was due to many difficulties, of both a mechanical and a chemical nature, in the manipulation of the cane and juice. The most important problems to be solved were the proper cutting and cleaning of the cane, the prevention of inversion of cane sugar in the diffusion battery, and to find a cheap and effective method for treating the diffusion juice.

PRELIMINARY EXPERIMENTS.

As soon as the earliest of the amber cane approached ripeness a large number of preliminary experiments were made in defecation and filtration of juices. The experiments in filtration were made with a small filter press with a hand pump. The cloth used was the same as that used in the large presses, and every precaution was taken to make the results just as valuable as if made on a larger scale. These experiments were begun on July 29. The filtering materials used were finely powdered lignite, bituminous coal, shale, several kinds of soils, and prepared carbonate of lime. The following conclusions were derived from these experiments :

(1) None of the above materials would filter juice satisfactorily that had an acid reaction.

(2) Neutral juice filtered very slowly and a hard-press cake would not form in the press.

(3) With a decidedly alkaline juice the filtration took place much more readily, but was not entirely satisfactory except with carbonate of lime.

(4) Lignite did not have any apparent decolorizing effect on the juice except when the juice had become highly colored by adding an excess of lime, when a slight decolorization took place. A large number of experiments were made with varying quantities of lignite, but in no case did it show any superiority over fine sandy loam, either as a decolorizer or filtering medium.

Experiments for testing the cutting, cleaning, and elevating machinery were also conducted as early as the condition of the cane would permit.

The method of unloading the cane and getting it onto the carrier was similar to that employed last year. The seed heads, however, were cut off in the field. The cutters were made by the Belle City Manufacturing Company, of Racine, Wis. They did the work well, but the machines were too light to stand the very severe work they were called upon to do.

The cane was cut into pieces about an inch long and then elevated by a drag to the top of a series of four fans standing straight over each other, each fan being furnished with a separate set of shakers. The cleaning apparatus, after considerable adjustment, did fairly good work. The leaves and sheaths were removed by a suction fan. The cleaned pieces of cane were cut by a rapidly revolving cutter, consisting of a cylinder carrying thirty knives. The cylinder was made up of three separate sections, each with ten knives. Although no difficulty was encountered in cutting, the work of the cutter was very unsatisfactory. A large portion of the chips consisted of long pieces with the bark on one side. Diffusion in this case could take place but in one direction, and in the largest chips of this kind the extraction of the sugar was very imperfect. The drag for conveying the chips to the cells was rebuilt and placed higher and on one side of the battery so as not to interfere with the packing of the chips in the cells. The exhausted chips were dumped directly into a car running on rails under the battery. This car was run up an incline onto a trestle work about 20 feet from the ground, by the aid of an endless cable. Two friction clutches, running in opposite directions, served to run the car forward or backward, and the car was so arranged that the charge of exhausted chips could be dropped at any point by simply reversing the motion of the cable.

EXPERIMENTS WITH CRUSHER.

It was the opinion of a number of men interested in this industry that a very much larger yield and better quality of juice could be obtained by the crushers if the cane, previously to being pressed, were cleaned and macerated, and it was deemed best to give the matter a thorough trial. For this purpose a 3-foot cane mill was purchased from J. A. Field & Co., of Saint Louis. It consisted of a three-roller mill and a supplemental two-roller mill. The principal trouble encountered was in feeding the mill. Even with an arrangement for forcing the chips between the rolls not over three tons per hour could be forced through, and the yield of juice was but little if any greater than when whole cane was fed to the mill.

The average yield of syrup was about 10 gallons per ton of cane worked. The same kind of cane yielded by diffusion 25 gallons of syrup per ton of cane. The cane used in this trial was very poor, being mostly lodged. These experiments show conclusively the great superiority of the diffusion process for syrup making, a very good quality of sirup being produced from very poor cane. It was superior in both color and flavor to the sirup from the mill juice. The juices from the mill and battery were treated precisely alike and they were skimmed and evaporated in an open steam evaporator. This is a matter of great importance to all engaged in the sugar business, as both at the beginning and close of the season there will be considerable cane that is not fit for sugar-making, and the fact that 25 gallons of first-class sirup can be made from such cane by diffusion makes it possible to work even such material at a good profit.

The first run for sugar was begun on August 26. The juice was made alkaline with lime, and about 2 per cent. of carbonate of lime was added. It was then filtered. To other portions of juice, instead of carbonate of lime, 3 per cent. of ground shale, bituminous coal, and sandy loam were added respectively. The filtrations were very imperfect except with the carbonate of lime and in every way corresponded with the preliminary experiments. Lignite was not used on a large scale because I had at the time no means of grinding it; but judging from a large number of experiments made in the beginning of the season, it is safe to conclude that it would not have filtered any better than the other materials used.

Satisfactory filtrations were only produced when the juice had been made strongly alkaline, and no material was found which would filter the juice when left slightly acid.

On August 30 the first strike was made, and the yield was a little more than 100 pounds of washed sugar per ton of clean cane.

INVERSION OF CANE SUGAR.

To prevent the inversion of the sugar in battery, about 10 pounds of dry precipitated carbonate of lime was mixed with enough water to produce a thin paste. This was added to the fresh chips while the cell was being filled, and entirely prevented any loss of sugar by inversion.

The carbonate was made by forcing carbonic acid gas by the aid of a pump into thin milk of lime. The injection pipe was perforated and lay along the bottom of a 10 by 10 feet tank containing the milk of lime. The gas was produced by burning coke in a small furnace. When the lime showed but a slight alkaline reaction it was run off into a large hole in the ground where the water soon drained away, leaving the carbonate nearly dry.

EXPERIMENTS WITH DEFECATION.

On September 1 filtration was dispensed with and experiments tried with simple defecation. The defecators were similar to those in ordinary use, being simply round tanks with conical bottoms and furnished with coils for heating the juice. This method of defecation, however, was not satisfactory, and defecation was tried in a shallow pan 16 feet long and 26 inches wide, with a partition running lengthwise in the center, the inlet and outlet for the juice being on the same end of the pan on opposite sides of the partition.

This pan was gotten up very hurriedly and was supplied with iron pipes for heating the juice. The juice, after being previously limed and somewhat heated, was pumped into one side of the long heating pan and run out at the opposite side continuously.

Being compelled by the center partition to flow down one side and back on the other, the juice made a circuit of 32 feet. The steam was so regulated that during the first 16 feet it was gradually brought to the boiling point, while in the opposite side it boiled vigorously. In this way a strong current was produced which carried all the impurities in the form of scum to the quiet portion of the juice, where it was removed and returned to the battery, thus avoiding all waste and annoyance from this source.

EVAPORATION.

The juice was evaporated to from 20° to 30° Baumé, in a double effect evaporator built by the Pusey & Jones Company, of Wilmington, Del. This apparatus gave perfect satisfaction. All the evaporation was done by exhaust steam of 4 pounds pressure, a small amount of live steam being used only when part of the machinery was stopped.

EXPERIMENTS IN BOILING TO GRAIN.

Every strike was boiled to grain in the pan. Several experiments were made to ascertain the result in boiling "in and in," the juice being enriched by the addition of sugar made from previous strikes. It is very doubtful, however, whether this is to be recommended, excepting when the juice is so poor that a good grain can not be obtained in any other way.

Owing to the fact that we were unable to secure a sufficient supply of cane the work progressed very irregularly. Only twice during the entire season was the battery kept in operation continuously for twenty hours, and during the sugar-making season the diffusion battery was emptied sixty-two times. This entailed no inconsiderable loss, amounting to from 1 to 2 tons of clean cane each time a stoppage occurred.

CANE WORKED FOR SUGAR.

The total amount of cane worked for sugar was 2,610 tons. In this is included all that was used for experiments in filtration and defecation during the first part of the season. I have no record of the exact amount lost in this way. The total amount of first sugar made was 235,476 pounds. This sugar was all washed, and polarized on an average 96 per cent. The total amount of molasses produced was 51,000 gallons.

TRIAL RUNS.

In order to ascertain as nearly as possible the average yield of sugar per ton of cane two trial runs were made.

FIRST TRIAL.

On September 15 a strike was made from 133 tons of clean cane. In order to obtain a better grain 2,600 pounds of sugar was added to the juice after it had been defecated; 2,200 pounds of juice were drawn from each cell.

The following is a record of this experiment:

Sucrose in mill, juice from chips	10.00
Glucose in mill, juice from chips	3.41
Solids not sugar, juice from chips	3.20
Ratio of sucrose to glucose	2.94
Coefficient of purity	60.3
Sucrose in diffusion juice	7.91
Glucose in diffusion juice	2.60
Solids not sugar, diffusion juice	2.59
Ratio of sucrose to glucose	3.04
Coefficient of purity	60.4
Sucrose in defecated juice	8.34
Glucose in defecated juice	2.40
Solids not sugar, defecated juice	2.46
Ratio of sucrose to glucose	3.47
Coefficient of purity	63.6
Total weight of first sugar ....pounds..	17,608
Sugar added to juice ....do....	2,600
Total yield first sugar ....do....	15,008
Total yield of second sugar ....do....	2,330
Total yield of molasses ....gallons..	2,220

Yield per ton :
```
    First sugar.......................................................................pounds..  113.00
    Second sugar ...................................................................do....   17.5
    Molasses ......................................................................gallons..   15.5
First sugar polarized ...............................................................   93.0
Second sugar polarized ..............................................................   88.7
```

Temperature in battery was between 75° and 80° C.

SECOND TRIAL.

Eighty-six tons of clean cane were worked; 54 tons on October 1, and 32 tons on October 2. All was boiled in one strike. No analyses were made on October 2, and unfortunately the complete data can not therefore be given. The juice was not enriched as in the previous trial.

The following are the results:
```
Yield of first sugar ...........................................................pounds..  9,292
Yield of second sugar ...........................................................do....  1,988
Yield of molasses................................................................gallons..  1,462
Yield per ton :
    First sugar.................................................................pounds..   108
    Second sugar ...............................................................do....   23
    Molasses ....................................................................gallons..   17
First sugar polarized ..............................................................   97
Second sugar polarized..............................................................   88
```

AVERAGE YIELD OF SUGAR.

Making a fair allowance for cane and juice lost in experiments during the first part of the season, the average yield of first sugars will be fully 100 pounds per ton, polarizing 97. A strike of average molasses boiled to string proof yielded 12½ per cent. of the weight of the *masse cuite* in sugar, containing 88 per cent. of sucrose. This is at the rate of 28 pounds per ton of cane. Had the entire crop been boiled for seconds the average yield per ton of cane would not have been less than 128 pounds of sugar and 16 gallons of molasses. From a financial standpoint the advantage of working for seconds depends entirely on the sirup market. In my judgment it would not have paid this season, as the market is better than for years past. The entire product of 51,000 gallons has already been sold at a good price.

AVAILABLE SUGAR.

It is at once apparent that the old method of calculating available sugar must be abandoned. According to this rule there would be but 61.6 pounds available sugar per ton of cane in the diffusion juice of the first trial, when as a matter of fact 130½ pounds was obtained. It would therefore seem that instead of preventing an equal weight of cane sugar from crystallizing, the glucose and other solids not sugar in the juice prevented only two-fifths of their weight of cane sugar from crystallizing. This is also borne out by the data furnished by the analysis of the juices during the entire season.

Average analyses from tables prepared by Dr. Crampton.

For week ending.	Mill juices.			Diffusion juices.			Total sugar (exhaust chips).
	Brix.	Sucrose.	Glucose.	Brix.	Sucrose.	Glucose.	
September 17	16.9	9.90	3.46	12.8	7.74	2.28	.99
September 24	17.3	9.63	3.52	12.2	6.88	2.35	.96
October 1	16.4	9.44	3.24	10.9	6.34	2.21	.63
October 9	16.4	9.96	3.36	11.0	6.60	2.31	.98
October 16	14.8	9.34	2.98	10.1	6.38	1.90	1.10
Average for season.	16.3	9.67	3.31	11.4	6.79	2.21	.93

Average ratio of sucrose to glucose in mill juices... 2.92
Average coefficient of purity of mill juices 59.3
Average ratio of sucrose to glucose in diffusion juices... 3.07
Average coefficient of purity of diffusion juices.. 59.5

The above table discloses two very important facts :

(1) The very uniform condition of the cane throughout the entire season.

(2) By the use of a small quantity of carbonate of lime in the cells the inversion of cane sugar is entirely prevented.

The amount of sugar left in the chips is larger than it ought to be. This is due, as previously stated, to the bad shape of some of the chips. For this reason the juice was also more dilute, as larger charges had to be drawn in order to get a more complete extraction. Up to September 22 the amount drawn was 2,200 pounds. From this to October 4 2,640 pounds, and from October 4 to the end of the season 2,420 pounds were drawn.

The temperature of the battery was maintained near 80°C.

EFFECT OF HEAT.

In order to determine the amount of inversion taking place when the juice was evaporated to sirup, in an open pan, the following experiments were made. Juice was boiled down in the open pan used for defecating, and samples taken at different intervals.

The following are the analyses:

Brix.	Sucrose.	Glucose.	Ratio of sucrose to glucose.
13.0	8.08	2.39	3.38
21.7	13.49	3.87	3.48
27.7	33.30	9.50	3.50
	37.20	11.36	3.27
	41.10	lost.	

[Trial on Potter's evaporator.]

Sucrose.	Glucose.	Ratio of sucrose to glucose.
6.71	2.04	3.44
30.20	11.80	3.32
50.00	15.26	3.21
51.00	15.88	3.21

The juice in both cases was made as nearly neutral with lime as possible.

It seems from the above that the invertive action of the heat has been greatly overestimated, and that when the juice is not acid no appreciable inversion takes place even when the juice is reduced to a moderately heavy sirup in an open pan.

From Mr. Parkinson's report it will be seen that the loss in leaves and sheaths amounted to about 11 per cent. of the weight of the topped cane. This loss can no doubt be somewhat reduced when the cleaning machines become better adapted to the work.

According to a number of trials with freshly cut cane the weight of leaves and sheaths amounted to 10 per cent. and the seed tops to 15 per cent. of the weight of the whole plant. Late in the season when the leaves become dry this proportion is of course considerably less.

COST OF A FACTORY.

A very important fact to determine is, the capacity and cost of a factory that will work the cane most economically. There can be no doubt but the advantages are greatly on the side of the large factory. The office expenses and cost of management will be but little, if any, greater. All the machinery required in a large factory is equally necessary in a small one and the proportionate price of this machinery is in favor of the larger factory. In other words, a factory working 200 tons of cane per day will cost much less than double the cost of a factory working 100 tons. Again, the cost of operating a large factory is proportionately much less. It takes no more men to operate a diffusion battery with a capacity of 200 tons of cane than one half as large, and this is true of the larger part of the machinery in the factory. A point may of course be reached where the size of the machinery becomes too large for economical working, and when the amount of cane needed for working will be greater than can be grown within easy reach of the factory.

Judging from our present knowledge, a factory capable of working from 200 to 250 tons of cleaned cane per day seems the most desirable. This would require a diffusion battery of 12 cells, each cell having a capacity of 112 cubic feet. The evaporating apparatus should have a capacity of 250 tons of water per day and a strike pan with a proportionate capacity. The cost of such machinery will, of course, depend largely on its kind and quality, and can be readily obtained from any reliable manufacturer. The cost of a factory is almost always underestimated, owing to many items which are not taken into account. The capital for building a factory of the above capacity should not be less than $100,000 to $125,000, any thing below being certainly unsafe. Nothing but the best machinery should be used and every precaution should be taken to prevent breakage of machinery and to be able to make repairs quickly by having duplicate parts of such machinery as are liable to break. There is no manufacture which depends more for its success on the proper working of the machinery than the sugar industry.

The success of this industry does not depend altogether on how much sugar can be produced per ton of cane, but the cost of this production must also be considered.

The success of the work during the past season has been largely due to the simplicity and cheapness of the processes employed. For the actual cost of production and other data of the utmost interest to those who contemplate engaging in this industry, I can not do better than refer them to the report of W. L. Parkinson to the board of directors of the Parkinson Sugar Company, which I have the permission to embody in this report. [1]

There is no doubt but that $2 per ton for working cane are sufficient to cover all legitimate expenses connected with the manufacture.

UTILIZATION OF THE EXHAUST CHIPS.

It will soon become a matter of necessity to dispose in some way of the exhausted chips from the battery.

The great amount of this material accumulating about the factory makes it imperative that they be utilized in some way. Three methods of disposition have been suggested : (1) To return them to the land as a fertilizer ; (2) to use them for fuel ; (3) to manufacture into paper pulp. One of the last two methods will no doubt be adopted. Some experiments in using for fuel were made during the season. A large portion of the water was pressed out by passing the chips through a 3-foot cane-crusher. The chips dropped from the last roll into a hopper, from which they were taken up by a suction-fan and blown over to the boiler-house. This method of handling the chips has many features to recommend it. It is very simple, and, besides, the chips are dried somewhat by being subjected to the strong current of air. No doubt the making of paper pulp from the chips will become the most profitable disposition to make of them. The cane after being reduced to fine chips and thoroughly washed in the diffusion battery is certainly in an excellent condition for this work. No attempts have been made, as far as I know, to make paper pulp on a large scale from this source, but very fine samples of pure white pulp have been made in a small way. This matter is certainly deserving of thorough investigation.

NEEDS OF THE INDUSTRY.

One of the greatest difficulties which will be encountered by those engaged in developing this industry will be the scarcity of men capable of operating factories. This will be the most serious hinderance to rapid

[1] See Cowgill's Report, p. 21.)

development, as nothing but time can produce men of the requisite experience. The establishment of a school for training young men in this work would be of inestimable value. Here they should receive thorough technical training, which should be supplemented with a drill in the factories while they are in operation. This would in a short time develop a number of men capable not only of taking charge of a factory, but also qualified to conduct independent research, which, in so fruitful a field, could not but result in great good to the industry.

The improvement of the sorghum cane is also one of the subjects which should receive immediate attention.

Although very little has been attempted in this line, enough has been done to show that the cane sugar is greatly increased by good culture, and that it is susceptible of very great improvement by the various methods known to scientific agriculture there can be no doubt. The idea that sorghum cane will grow anywhere and do well with any kind of treatment is one of the main causes of poor cane. Instead of receiving thorough culture, it generally gets only such attention as can be spared from the other crops. If the price paid for cane could be regulated by the actual amount of sugar it contained, the farmer would soon find it to his advantage to devote more time to his cane field.

The establishment of a sugar refinery within easy reach of the sorghum-sugar factories will be one of the imperative needs in the near future. The demand for any kind of sugar but white granulated is comparatively limited. The sugar produced at Fort Scott averaged within $2\frac{1}{2}$ per cent. of being as pure as the best granulated, while the selling price has been about $1\frac{1}{2}$ cents per pound less, or a difference of about 25 per cent. The most feasible manner of conducting the refinery, at least in the near future, will be to supply one or more factories with the additional appliances needed, and when the season's work is over the sugar from a number of factories could be refined there during the balance of the year.

Before closing this report I wish to extend my thanks to Mr. W. L. Parkinson, manager of the Parkinson Sugar Company, for his hearty co-operation. The successful handling, cutting, and cleaning the cane were due to the results of his thought and labor.

I also desire to express my appreciation of the faithful and valuable services rendered by my assistants, Messrs. J. O. Hart and J. N. Wilcox; and my thanks are due Dr. C. A. Crampton and Mr. N. J. Fake, chemists of the U. S. Department of Agriculture, for aid and courtesies extended.

CONCLUSIONS.

In reviewing the work the most important point suggested is the complete success of the experiments in demonstrating the commercial practicablity of manufacturing sugar from sorghum cane.

(2) That sugar was produced uniformly throughout the entire season.

(3) That this was not due to any extraordinary content of sugar in the cane, but, on the contrary, the cane was much injured by severe drought and chinch-bugs.

(4) That the value of the sugar and molasses obtained this year per ton of sorghum cane will compare favorably with that of the highest yields obtained in Louisiana from sugar-cane, and, taking into consideration the much greater cost of the sugar-cane, and that it has no equivalent to the 2 bushels of seed yielded per ton of sorghum cane, also our much cheaper fuel, I say without hesitancy that sugar can be produced fully as cheaply in Kansas as in Louisiana.

M. SWENSON.

SUMMARY OF CHEMICAL WORK DONE AT FORT SCOTT, 1887.

[Abstract of report of C. A. Crampton.]

Analyses were begun on the 3d of September, but a full chemical control of the work was not established until the 8th.

Samples of the fresh chips, diffusion juices, and exhausted chips were taken in the usual way, great care being taken to have them represent as accurately as possible the mean properties of the several substances mentioned.

TABLE 1.—Analyses of juices of fresh chips.

Number of analyses	55
Sucrose :	Per cent
Mean	9.54
Maximum	11.51
Minimum	6.20
Glucose :	
Mean	3.40
Maximum	6.49
Minimum	1.39
Total solids (spindle):	
Mean	16.14
Maximum	17.18
Minimum	13.09

TABLE 2.—Diffusion juices.

Number of analyses	51
Sucrose :	Per cent.
Mean	6.68
Maximum	8.79
Minimum	5.05
Glucose :	
Mean	2.26
Maximum	3.07
Minimum	1.75
Total solids (spindle) :	
Mean	11.08
Maximum	13.10
Minimum	8.64

TABLE 3.—*Exhausted chips.*

Number of analyses 29
Both sugars: Per cent.
  Mean 1. 03
  Maximum 1. 83
  Minimum .... .49

TABLE 4.—*Clarified juices.*

Number of analyses 25
Sucrose: Per cent.
  Mean 6. 91
  Maximum 8. 25
  Minimum 5. 11
Glucose:
  Mean 2. 19
  Maximum 2. 85
  Minimum 1. 69
Total solids (spindle):
  Mean 11. 31
  Maximum 13. 35
  Minimum 8. 94

TABLE 5.—*Sirups.*

Number of analyses 14
Sucrose: Per cent.
  Mean 29. 90
  Maximum 41. 90
  Minimum 16. 10
Glucose:
  Mean 10. 06
  Maximum 16. 26
  Minimum 7. 52
Total solids (spindle):
  Mean 46. 02
  Maximum 60. 40
  Minimum 36. 20

TABLE 6.—*First sugars.*

Number of analyses 28
Sucrose: Per cent.
  Mean 95. 64
  Maximum 98. 10
  Minimum 92. 40

TABLE 7.—*Second sugars.*

Number of analyses 3
Sucrose: Per cent.
  Mean 85. 80
  Maximum 88. 70
  Minimum 82. 30

The analyses of the molasses, masse cuites, and some other products are not yet complete, but will be given in full in Bulletin No. 18.

The ratio of sucrose to glucose in the fresh chips and diffusion juices for the season was as follows:

Mill juice .... 1 : 2. 80
Diffusion juice .... 1 : 2. 95

This would seem to show one of two things, either that there was absolutely no inversion in the battery or that the glucose in the cane was not so readily diffused as the sucrose. The latter hypothesis seems to be borne out by the analyses of the exhausted chips as shown in the following table of analyses:

Sucrose and glucose in juice from exhausted chips and corresponding diffusion juices.

Date.	Exhausted chips.			Diffusion juices.		
	No.	Sucrose.	Glucose.	No.	Sucrose.	Glucose.
		Per cent.	Per cent.		Per cent.	Per cent.
Oct. 8	248	.78	.57	247	5.90	3.06
Oct. 11	200	.87	.51	250	6.58	2.00
Oct. 12	267	.63	.29	266	6.17	2.03
Oct. 13	280	.95	.48	279	5.07	1.89
Oct. 14	289	.52	.24	288	6.02	1.80
Oct. 15	294	.75	.27	293	5.66	1.75
Oct. 18	313	.90	.43	312	5.66	2.02
Average	....	.78	.40	....	5.99	2.09

15449—No. 17——2

THE SORGHUM-SUGAR INDUSTRY IN KANSAS.*

REPORT OF E. B. COWGILL.

OFFICE OF THE STATE BOARD OF AGRICULTURE,
Topeka, Kans., December 17, 1887.

While all attempts to manufacture sugar from sorghum in Kansas had, prior to the present season, resulted in disappointment and financial disaster, confidence was not destroyed. The failures of the past, and the obstacles to success, which many of large experience had declared to be insurmountable, seemed only to nerve those whose confidence in the final success of the industry remained unshaken, to renewed and more determined effort. Congress had been induced to provide means to aid in the further prosecution of experimental work, but capital was required to enable Kansas to avail herself of the assistance offered. Those having the greatest financial interest in the industry were generally discouraged, and individuals having nothing at risk could hardly be expected to invest in so unpromising an enterprise.

Under these circumstances the legislature was appealed to, and on March 5, 1887, "an act to encourage the manufacture of sugar" was secured, which provides: First, that a bounty of two cents per pound shall be paid upon all sugar manufactured in this State from beets, sorghum, or other sugar-yielding canes or plants grown in Kansas. Second, that no bounty shall be paid upon sugar containing less than 90 per cent. of crystallized sugar, the quantity and quality to be determined by the secretary of the State board of agriculture, or other person appointed by him, the cost of such inspection to be borne by the claimant. Third, the sum of money so to be paid shall not exceed in any one year $15,000.

The secretary of the board, recognizing his inability to perform the duties imposed by the act above referred to, did, on the 15th day of August, 1887, by virtue of the authority in him vested, appoint and commission Prof. E. B. Cowgill inspector, under the provisions of said act, and authorized and empowered him to do and perform, all and singular, the duties as such inspector; also to make such observation and

---

* This report has been corrected by the author, several errors having been overlooked in the advance sheets.

investigation of the means and methods employed in the manufacture of sugar as the public interest might seem to require; and to report to this office, as required by law, and indicated in the instructions transmitted with said commission, as follows:

STATE BOARD OF AGRICULTURE,
Topeka, Kans., August 15, 1887.

DEAR SIR: In inspecting sugar, on which bounty is claimed under the act of the legislature approved March 5, 1887, and in your observations of processes, and in investigating the subject of sugar making in Kansas under the commission herewith presented, you will observe the following instructions:

I. In accordance with section 2 of said act, you will proceed to inspect sugar made in Kansas when called upon by the manufacturers, and,

First, determine the percentage of crystallized sugar, uncrystallized sugar, and of substances not sugar, contained in each package presented for inspection.

Second, keep a full and correct record of the quantities and qualities of sugar on which bounty is claimed.

II. In determining the quality of sugars you will make analyses by the copper reduction, or such other method or methods as you may deem best.

III. You will weigh and brand all sugars inspected, and keep possession of the same until delivered or consigned to purchaser, and you will keep a correct record of each delivery and consignment: *Provided,* That you may permit delivery and shipments to be made, during your absence from the works, by some person to be designated by you, who shall keep a full and correct record of such delivery and consignment, and present to you a sworn statement of the same, together with receipts of purchaser or transportation companies.

IV. You shall also take such sworn testimony of manufacturers, employés, station agents, or consignees, and such other evidence as shall fully determine the quantity of the sugar to be reported for payment of bounty.

V. When the entire product of the season at any factory has been inspected, and your record completed as above directed, you will transmit to this office a sworn statement, showing the quality and quantity of sugars made by said factory, and will turn over to the manufacturers all unsold products.

VI. You will observe processes and experiments, and make investigations as opportunities permit, and report fully to this office, to the end that the people of the State may have the advantage of all information gained and processes developed under the encouragement of the bounty provided in the act above referred to.

Yours truly,

WM. SIMS,
Secretary State Board of Agriculture.

Prof. E. B. COWGILL,
Sterling, Kans.

The appointment above referred to was, on the 21st day of August, 1887, duly accepted by Professor Cowgill, who filed herein his oath of office, and at once entered upon the duties of his said appointment, and who, on the 7th day of December, 1887, delivered to the secretary of the board his report, as such inspector, showing the quantity and quality of sugar contained in each of the packages presented for inspection, and on which bounty was claimed and is now due under the provisions of the act of March 5, 1887, above referred to.

This report shows 842 packages, containing 234,607 pounds of sugar, to have been inspected and branded as provided by law, and that the packages so inspected contained from 92 to 98 per cent. of crystallized sugar, respectively.

The amount claimed as bounty, and due thereon from the State treasury, is $4,692.14, leaving of the appropriation for 1887, above referred to, unclaimed, the sum of $10,307.86.

And afterwards, to wit, on the 15th day of December, 1887, there was filed in this office, by Professor Cowgill, his complete and final report relating to the sorghum-sugar industry in Kansas, which is herewith submitted for the information of the public.

WM. SIMS,
Secretary.

LETTER OF TRANSMITTAL.

SIR: Under commission from your office dated August 15, 1887, and instructions to inspect and brand sugars made in this State during the season of 1887, as provided in the act of the legislature approved March 5, 1887, and under your further instructions to ascertain whether sugar-making in Kansas is a success or a failure, and why, I proceeded to the Parkinson Sugar Works, at Fort Scott, the only sugar factory in operation in the State, and inspected and branded the sugar produced, as set forth in detail in Exhibit A. I also made a careful study of the processes used, and submit herewith my report. I am aware that much that is contained in the following pages is not new to those familiar with the usual methods of making sugar; but realizing that to most of those who will read this report the details of the entire subject are new, I have deemed it proper to describe the old as well as the new in the processes employed in the manufacture as at present conducted. I have not hoped to enable persons unfamiliar with the subject to at once enter upon the profitable manufacture of sugar, but to help those who are studying the subject, and to place reliable information on a most important new industry within the reach of the intelligent Kansas public.

I am, sir, yours respectfully,

E. B. COWGILL.

Hon. WM. SIMS,
 Secretary State Board of Agriculture.

REPORT OF E. B. COWGILL.

HISTORICAL SKETCH.

The sorghum plant was introduced into the United States in 1853–'54 by the Patent Office, which then embraced all there was of the United States Department of Agriculture. Its juice was known to be sweet, and chemists were not long in discovering that it contained a considerable percentage of some substance giving the reactions of cane sugar. The opinion that the reactions were due to cane sugar received repeated confirmations in the formation of true cane-sugar crystals in sirups made from sorghum. Yet the small amounts that were crystallized, compared with the amounts present in the juices as shown by the analyses, led many to believe that the reactions were largely due to some other substance than cane sugar.

EARLY INVESTIGATIONS OF THE UNITED STATES DEPARTMENT OF AGRICULTURE.

During the years 1878 to 1882, inclusive, while Dr. Peter Collier was chief chemist of the Department of Agriculture, much attention was given to the study of sorghum juices from canes cultivated in the gardens of the Department, at Washington. Dr. Collier became an enthusiastic believer in the future greatness of sorghum as a sugar-producing plant, and the extensive series of analyses published by him attracted much attention from sugar-makers in the South, and students of the chemistry of sugar throughout the country.

SUGAR FACTORIES ERECTED IN KANSAS.

Stimulated by the analytical results published by Dr. Collier, interested parties erected large sugar factories and provided them with costly appliances. Hon. John Bennyworth erected one of these at Larned, in this State. S. A. Liebold & Co. subsequently erected one at Great Bend. Both of these factories made some sugar, both lost money, and both quit the business.

Sterling and Hutchinson followed with factories which made considerable amounts of merchantable sugar at no profit.

The factory at Sterling was erected by R. M. Sandys & Co., of New Orleans, who sought, by combining Mr. Sandys' thorough knowledge of

21

sugar with the best practical skill of the South, to establish the sorghum-sugar industry on a proper basis. For two seasons this combination worked faithfully, and while the sirup produced paid the expenses of the factory, not a crystal of sugar was made. The factory then in 1883 changed hands, and passed under the superintendency of Prof. M. A. Scovell, then of Champaign, Ill., who, with Professor Weber, had worked out, in the laboratories of the Illinois Industrial University, a practical method for obtaining sugar from sorghum in quantities which at prices then prevalent would pay a profit on the business. But prices declined, and after making sugar for two years in succession the Sterling factory succumbed.

The Hutchinson factory at first made no sugar, but subsequently passed under the management of Prof. M. Swenson, who had success-fully made sugar in the laboratory of the University of Wisconsin. Large amounts of sugar were made at a loss, and the Hutchinson factory closed its doors. In 1884 Hon. W. L. Parkinson fitted up a complete sugar factory at Ottawa, and for two years made sugar at a loss. Mr. Parkin-son was assisted during the first year by Dr. Wilcox, and during the second year by Professor Swenson.

INFORMATION GAINED.

Much valuable information was developed by the experience in these several factories, but the most important of all was the fact that, with the best crushers, the average extraction did not exceed half of the sugar contained in the cane. It was known to scientists and well-in-formed sugar-makers in this country that the process of diffusion was theoretically efficient for the extraction of sugar from plant cells, and that it had been successfully applied by the beet-sugar-makers of Europe for this purpose.

FURTHER WORK OF THE U. S. DEPARTMENT OF AGRICULTURE.

In 1883, Prof. H. W. Wiley, chief chemist of the Department of Agri-culture, made an exhaustive series of practical experiments in the lab-oratories of the Department on the extraction of the sugars from sorghum by the diffusion process. His report sums up the results of his experi-ments as follows:

(1) The extraction of at least 85 per cent. of the total sugars present was secured. In many of the experiments, as will be seen by consulting the table, scarcely a trace of sugar could be detected in the exhausted chips.

(2) The production of a quantity of melada represented by from 10.9 to 12.28 per cent. of the weight of the cane diffused.

This was secured with a cane in which the total sugars did not exceed 11.68 per cent. The percentage of melada by this process will be found just about equal to the per cent. of total sugars in the cane.

It ought to be greater with a more perfect extraction, but I am speaking only of results actually obtained.

This yield is just about double that obtained by the large factories at Rio Grande, Champaign, and other places.

(3) The production of a juice of great purity, which lends itself easily to processes of depuration.

I consider the experiments, however, to have their chief value in the fact that they will call the attention of cane-growers to the advantages which a rational system of diffusion will have over pressure in the extraction of the saccharine matter.

I hope to be able at the end of another season to report further progress in this interesting problem.

In the present condition of the sorghum-sugar industry, in which it has alike to be protected from the over-zeal of its friends and the opposition of its enemies, the process of diffusion offers the most promising outlook for success. It therefore seems the duty of this division to make a more practical test of this process and on a larger scale.

To make the necessary further experiments with diffusion, required the expenditure of large sums of money. As already shown, the private companies had lost heavily. They were utterably unable to complete the experiments so hopefully begun by the Department of Agriculture.

THE AID OF CONGRESS SOLICITED.

At this crisis Hon. W. L. Parkinson and Mr. Alfred Taylor, of Ottawa, Kans., after consulting with others interested in the then languishing sorghum-sugar industry, went to Washington to call the attention of Congress to the important results promised for the diffusion process, and to show that, without the aid of an appropriation, all that had hitherto been accomplished would be practically lost. The Kansas delegation in Congress became interested. Senator Plumb made a thorough study of the entire subject, and, with the foresight of statesmanship, gave his energies to the work of securing an appropriation of $50,000 for the development of the sugar industry. This appropriation was made during the last days of the session of 1884. The season was too far advanced to erect and use the diffusion apparatus with sorghum cane, and it was, by the Commissioner of Agriculture, sent to Louisiana, and sorghum got no benefit from this first appropriation.

ANOTHER APPROPRIATION.

In 1885, Senator Plumb, at the request of Judge Parkinson, Professor Swenson, and others, again labored for an appropriation for experiments with diffusion. It was shown by Judge Parkinson, and all others interested in the sorghum-sugar industry, that this was the only hope for success. Fifty thousand dollars for this purpose was again added to the agricultural appropriation bill, on the amendment of Senator Plumb. This was expended at Ottawa, Kans., and in Louisiana. The report of the work at Ottawa closes as follows:

(1) By the process of diffusion 98 per cent. of the sugar in the cane was extracted, and the yield was fully double that obtained in the ordinary way.

(2) The difficulties to be overcome in the application of diffusion are wholly mechanical. With the apparatus on hand the following changes are necessary in order to be able to work 120 tons per day: (a) The diffusion cells should be made twice as

large as they now are; that is, of 130 cubic feet capacity. (*b*) The opening through which the chips are discharged should be made as nearly as possible of the same area as a horizontal cross-section of the cell. (*c*) The forced feed of the cutters requires a few minor changes in order to prevent choking. (*d*) The apparatus for delivering the chips to the cells should be remodeled so as to dispense with the labor of one man.

(3) The process of carbonatation for the purification of the juice is the only method which will give a limpid juice with a minimum of waste and a maximum of purity.

(4) By a proper combination of diffusion and carbonatation the experiments have demonstrated that fully 95 per cent. of the sugar in the cane can be placed on the market either as dry sugar or molasses.

(5) It is highly important that the Department complete the experiments so successfully inaugurated by making the changes in the machinery mentioned above and by the erection of a complete carbonatation outfit.

Respectfully,

H. W. WILEY, *Chemist*.

But while so much had been accomplished by the joint efforts of the United States Department of Agriculture and the Ottawa company, the financial results were so disastrous to the company as to leave them utterly unable to further co-operate with the Government in the prosecution of the work.

THE FORT SCOTT COMPANY ORGANIZED.

At this juncture Judge Parkinson saw that he must either submit to defeat or organize a new company to co-operate with the Department of Agriculture, should Congress be wise enough to make another appropriation. In this straight he went to Fort Scott and organized the Parkinson Sugar Company, which is now composed as follows: J. D. Hill, president; Eli Kearnes, vice-president; M. Swenson, secretary and chemist; W. Chenault, treasurer; W. L. Parkinson, manager; O. F. Drake, A. W. Walburn, W. W. Pusey, J. W. Converse, and David Richards.

Taking up the work where all others had failed, this company has taken a full share of the responsibilities and losses, until it has at last seen the Northern sugar industry made a financial success.

THE HOUSE OF REPRESENTATIVES MAKES AN APPROPRIATION.

The report of 1885 showed such favorable results that in 1886 the House made an appropriation of $94,000, to be used in Louisiana, New Jersey, and Kansas. A new battery and complete carbonatation apparatus were erected at Fort Scott. About $60,000 of the appropriation was expended here in experiments in diffusion and carbonatation.

In his report Dr. Wiley arrived at the following conclusions:

In a general review of the work, the most important point suggested is the absolute failure of the experiments to demonstrate the commercial practicability of manufacturing sorghum sugar. The causes of this failure have been pointed out in the preceding pages, and it will only be necessary here to recapitulate them. They were:

(1) Defective machinery for cutting the canes and for elevating and cleaning the chips and for removing the exhausted chips.

(2) The deterioration of the cane due to much of it becoming over-ripe, but chiefly to the fact that much time would generally elapse after the canes were cut before they reached the diffusion battery. The heavy frost which came the first of October also injured the cane somewhat, but not until ten days or two weeks after it occurred.

(3) The deteriorated cane caused a considerable inversion of the sucrose in the battery, an inversion which was increased by the delay in furnishing chips, thus causing the chips in the battery to remain exposed under pressure for a much longer time than was necessary. The mean time required for diffusing one cell was twenty-one minutes, three times as long as it should have been.

(4) The process of carbonatation, as employed, secured a maximum yield of sugar, but failed to make a molasses which was marketable. This trouble arose from the small quantity of lime remaining in the filtered juices, causing a blackening of the sirup on concentration, and the failure of the cleaning apparatus to properly prepare the chips for diffusion.

THE COMMISSIONER OF AGRICULTURE DISCOURAGED.

After the expenditure of so much money, and the publication of so discouraging a report as that of 1886, the Commissioner of Agriculture declined to ask for further appropriations.* But Senator Plumb again came to the rescue, and, by a faithful presentation of the possibilities of the case, induced Congress to make an appropriation of $50,000, of which $24,000 was apportioned to Louisiana, $6,000 to Rio Grande, N. J., and $20,000 to Fort Scott, Kans.†

SUCCESS AT LAST.

This year the Fort Scott management made careful selection of essential parts of the processes already used, omitted non-essential and cumbrous processes, availed themselves of all the experience of the past in this country, and secured a fresh infusion of experience from the beet-sugar factories of Germany, and attained the success which finally places sorghum sugar-making among the profitable industries of the country.

STATE ENCOURAGEMENT.

The State of Kansas had, by all reports, been indicated as the center of the sorghum-sugar industry, when it should be developed. Kansas statesmen in the legislature, as early as 1885, conceded that the State should assist in the development of the new industry. In that year Hon. R. F. Bond, member of the house from Rice County, prepared and introduced a bill providing for a bounty of 1½ cents per pound, to be paid out of the State treasury, on all sugar manufactured in the State

* The non-action of the Commissioner is misunderstood by Mr. Cowgill. When the House Committee on Agriculture made the appropriation of the preceding year it was agreed that no subsequent grant should be demanded. It was in harmony with this agreement and not for the reasons stated that the Commissioner did not ask for a further appropriation.

† The distribution of the money to the various stations was left to the discretion of the Commissioner, and was not mentioned in the bill.

for five years. The bill awakened a great deal of enthusiasm, and, at the same time, a factious opposition, and was lost. At the session of 1887 Senator Bawden, of Bourbon County, introduced a bill providing for a bounty of 2 cents per pound, to be paid upon all sugar manufactured in the State for five years, the maximum amount to be paid in any year being limited to $15,000. This bill became a law.

It will thus be seen that the present condition of the sorghum-sugar industry is due to private enterprise, aided by Government and State appropriations, and directed by scientific and practical skill.

COMMISSIONERS OF AGRICULTURE LE DUC, LORING, AND COLMAN.

It should be mentioned in this connection that United States Commissioner of Agriculture Le Duc extended a strong and friendly hand to the sorghum-sugar industry during his term of office. His successor, Commissioner Loring, had the work continued by Professor Wiley, but was himself skeptical as to results. The present Commissioner, Hon. Norman J. Colman, had been an advocate of sorghum for many years before his accession to office, and had probably written and published more on the subject than any other man in the United States. Every friend of the struggling industry was gratified at his appointment. He has extended all the aid at his command, and may justly feel proud of the attainment of the present success under his administration of the Department of Agriculture.

THE PRESENT STATE OF THE INDUSTRY.

The experiments in making sugar from sorghum, which, as above shown, have been in progress for several years at the expense of private capital and the United States Department of Agriculture, have this year reached so favorable results as to place the manufacture of sorghum sugar on the basis of a profitable business, as will be seen by the report to his company of Hon. W. L. Parkinson, manager of the Fort Scott works.

The success has been due to, first, the almost complete extraction of the sugars from the cane by the diffusion process; second, the prompt and proper treatment of the juice in defecating and evaporating; third, the efficient manner in which the sugar was boiled to grain in the strike-pan. That these results may be duplicated and improved upon will be readily understood from the showing made in Mr. Parkinson's report, and the descriptions of methods and processes used, and the discussion of the same as they appear in the subsequent pages of this paper.

REPORT OF W. L. PARKINSON.

To the Board of Directors Parkinson Sugar Company:

GENTLEMEN: I respectfully submit for your consideration the following report of the operations of the works of your company for the season just closing:

It is provided in our contract with the United States Department of Agriculture that certain experiments in sugar-making shall be made by the Department with certain machinery of its own and at its own expense, using the company's plant and machinery. Many of those experiments have been so closely allied to and dovetailed into the regular work of the factory that it is very difficult, if not wholly impossible, to clearly separate the cost of the experimental work from that of the general operation of the factory during the season. At the same time it is highly important that you know as precisely as possible the cost of working and the profit or loss on each ton of cane handled.

As you are aware, the crop of cane contracted for last spring was very much less than the capacity of our works to consume. It was considered prudent to limit our danger from loss, by reason of the experimental nature of the work, and at the same time to have sufficient cane to determine thoroughly the value of the work on a practical manufacturing basis. This has been done, though it is now apparent that had the crop been twice as large, the expenses for working it would have been relatively much less. Indeed, a crop double the size of the one just finished could have been worked in about the same time, and at a comparatively trifling additional expense. The plans, methods, and processes which have made the work of the season successful beyond our most sanguine expectations, were adopted early in the season, so that the risks incident to experiments taken into account when contracting for a crop were reduced to the minimum. The fact that at least a portion of these highly successful processes were not tried and adopted last season was no fault of your company, nor of any one connected with this season's work.

To arrive at the cost per ton of cane worked, let us take the working of a single average day, when in full operation, and apart from the cost of experiments referred to.

The capacity of our factory, aside from deficient centrifugals, is limited to the capacity of the diffusion battery. Working twenty-two hours per day, this battery can comfortably handle 135 tons of chips, or cleaned cane. This represents a capacity of field cane, or cane with seed tops and blades, of about 170 tons. To handle this, aside from curing and handling seed, cost us per day of twenty-two hours, when running regularly, as follows:

1 weighmaster, at $2	$2.00
1 team, pulling cane onto storage racks, at $2.50	2.50
5 men, unloading and getting cane to cutters, 22 hours, at 12¼ cents	13.75
1 man, cutting machine, at 15 cents	3.30
1 man, cleaning machine, at 12½ cents	2.75
1 man, grinder, etc., at 15 cents	3.30
1 man, oiler, at 15 cents	3.30
3 men, diffusion battery, 1 at car and 2 above, at 12½ cents	8.25
1 man, diffusion battery, director of battery, at 20 cents	4.40
2 men, defecating, at 15 cents	6.60
2 men, double effects, at 15 cents	6.60
1 man, strike-pan, at $5	5.00
1 man, hot room, at 12½ cents	2.75
1 man, barreler, at 12½ cents	2.75
2 men, centrifugals, at 15 cents	6.60
1 man, machinist, at $3	3.00
2 men, engineers, at 20 cents	4.40
5 men, firemen, at 15 cents	16.50
2 men, roustabouts, at 12½ cents	5.50
1 man, water boy	2.00
1 man, night watch	1.50
2 men, foremen, at $2.50	5.00
Total cost of labor	111.75
Oil, etc	2.50
Coal, 23 tons slack, at 90 cents	20.70

This makes the cost of working a ton of cleaned cane, with a factory of the capacity of ours, about $1 per ton for labor and fuel, or 90 cents per ton of field cane. The cost per ton for salaries, insurance, wear and tear, etc., must depend, of course, not only upon the size of the salaries and other general expenses, but the number of tons worked. This plant, rated as above, is capable, in seventy days, of working 9,450 tons of chips, or 11,900 tons of field cane. There is necessarily considerable expense in preparing for the season's work, and again in closing up. Allowing liberally for this and for the proper management and control of the works, we may still bring our total expenses, outside the cost of labor and fuel, at $1 per ton upon the above basis. Add to this the cost of labor and fuel, and we have $2 per ton as the total cost per ton of working cleaned cane. These figures are fully verified by our pay-rolls, coal bills, and other expenses while working to our capacity during the season, separated from expenditures in the completion and changing of machinery directly connected with experiments made. And to work a factory with a capacity at least one-half greater than this one would require very little additional expense except in the matter of fuel, and that would be relatively less. It seems to me a very conservative basis, with a factory of the capacity of ours, to place the actual cost of manafacture at $2 per ton of cane; and with such a factory as I have indicated, and with a season of, say, seventy days, it is safe to place the cost of manufacture at considerably less than that sum. It requires but little figuring upon this basis, and with the cost of cane at $2 per ton, and the yield of cane and product secured this year, to show that we have here developed a business of great interest and profit to our State and Nation.

To run a factory at the maximum profit it must be operated constantly during the working season. The loss this season by reason of the irregular operation of the factory for want of sufficient cane was very consideraole. During the whole season the factory was operated but three whole days of twenty-two hours each. Some idea of the loss from this source may be gathered from the fact that not less than 2 tons of chips were lost at each break in the operation of the diffusion battery. Sixty-five such breaks or stoppages were made while running for sugar. With a larger crop of cane and better arrangements for delivery upon the part of the larger contractors, but little or no difficulty from this source need be apprehended in the future.

	Tons.
Total cane bought	3,840
Total seed tops bought	437
Total field cane	4,277

This represents the crop, less about 30 tons of seed tops yet to come in, from about 450 acres of land. There were something over 500 acres planted. Some of it failed to come at all, some "fell upon the rocky places, where they had not much earth, and when the sun was risen they were scorched;" so that, as nearly as we can estimate, about 450 acres of cane were actually harvested and delivered at the works. This would make the average yield of cane 9½ tons per acre, or $19 per acre in dollars and cents. I beg to observe, in this connection, that the present was the lightest in tonnage of the five successive crops I have handled. It was probably also the poorest in crystallizable sugar, covering the same period of time, in the State. It may not be amiss to observe, too, in this connection, that a very commonly accepted theory, that "the dryer the weather the sweeter the cane," is not verified by my experience.

Of the total cane worked, 162 tons were consumed in experiments with our cutters and cleaning machinery before the cane was ripe enough for use for either sirup or sugar. No product whatever, not even seed, was saved from this, nor from 10 tons additional brought in since the factory closed down. About 300 tons of mostly down and inferior cane was worked in the early part of the season on the crushers, and without diffusion. The only product from this was molasses, and of that but a small quantity. About 375 tons were also worked for molasses only on the diffusion battery. This, with the exception of 50 tons at the close of the season, and which came in too irregularly to be worked for sugar, was worked before the sugar season began, and comprised such down patches and poorer quality of cane as could bo gathered, mainly on the lands belonging to the company. It was an open question whether very poor cane could be worked successfully, even for sirups, on a diffusion battery. Nothing in this direction had hitherto been attempted. The total yield of molasses from this source, and from which no sugar has been taken, is 4,157 gallons. From this are sold 3,157 gallons, for $726.71 net. The remaining 1,000 gallons are still on hand, and are worth 25 cents per gallon.

	Tons.
Deducting from total tonnage, less seed...	3,840
Amount not worked for sugar	897
We have total cane and leaves for sugar................................	2,943

The total number of diffusion cells worked for sugar is 2,643. The weight of a cell of chips is 1,975 pounds. With this as a basis there was worked by diffusion for sugar 2,610 tons of clean cane as it entered the cells. Deducting this from 2,943 tons of cane, with leaves and blades, and we have 333 tons of leaves and blades. The latter are to us a dead loss. A small portion has been hauled away by farmers for feed, but the bulk of this large tonnage is now fit only for manure. This waste was considerably increased by the failure of our separating machines, especially in the early part of the season, to properly discharge their duties. This whole subject was new ; machines had to be devised, and their adjustment, which is not yet perfect, caused considerable loss of cane. The weight of blades and leaves will not be far from 10 per cent. of field cane. For either feed or fuel, especially where the latter is much of an object, the blades can be utilized so as to at least cover their own cost. At present we figure the loss from this source to seed account.

SEED.

There have been delivered of seed tops 437 tons. As nearly as we can estimate, there are yet to be delivered 30 tons, making in all 467 tons. From the best calculations we can make, and judging from our experience in former years, seed yields about 70 per cent. of the weight of heads, as bought in over the scales, in cleaned seed. Putting it at 60 per cent., and with 56 pounds to the bushel, we shall have 10,000 bushels of cleaned seed. A portion of this, estimated at 1,000 bushels, has, at considerable additional expense, been picked over by hand, head by head, tied into small bundles, and hung up in the dry. This has been done to provide ourselves with pure seed of the different varieties for planting, and to supply a probable want in the same direction from others. For this hand-picked seed we expect to get not less than $2 per bushel. The cost of handling the seed has not been kept separate from the cost of running the factory. The total cost of curing, stacking, and hand-picking will not be far from $700, fully $200 of which has been expended in securing pure and perfectly cured seed for ourselves and others willing to pay the extra price. To thrash and prepare the seed for market the seed will cost about 6 cents per bushel additional. I estimate that we shall get for our seed crop $7,000 net. There will be left of seed tops, after thrashing, fully 100 tons. These are good for feed or fuel.

SIRUPS.

The bulk of our sirups are stored in the large cistern or cellar under the warehouse. The amount on hand we estimate at 50,000 gallons. This includes the whole crop, except the 3,157 gallons sold in early part of season. Of this we have sold, to be delivered within thirty days, and one car-load of which has already gone, 250 barrels, or about 12,500 gallons, at a price that will net us here 20 cents. This sale includes the bulk of our poorest sirups. I think we can safely estimate our sirup product, exclusive of packages, at $10,000. Considering the condition of our factory for work in cold weather, and the limited capacity of our centrifugal machinery, I recommend their sale, without boiling, for seconds.

SUGAR.

Of our sugar product, the State inspector, Prof. E. B. Cowgill, has weighed and certified for State bounty 206,326 pounds. We have now in addition and ready for inspection 22,500 pounds. The centrifugals are still running. We estimate that we shall still have, exclusive of seconds, from 7,000 to 10,000 pounds, or, in all, 235,826 pounds. This, at 5¾ cents, present price to jobbers, will produce us $13,559.98. To this add the State bounty of 2 cents per pound, and we have for our total sugar product $17,276.50.

TOTAL PRODUCT OF THE SEASON.

*Sugar, 235,826 pounds, at 5¾ cents	$13,559.98
Sugar, State bounty, at 2 cents	4,716.52
	17,276.50
Sirups, 51,000 gallons (estimated), at 20 cents	10,200.00
Seed (estimated)	7,000.00
Value of total product	34,476.50

TOTAL COST.

Cane, 3,840 tons, at $2	7,680.00
Seed, 967 tons, at $2	1,934.00
	9,614.00
Labor bill from August 15 to October 15, including labor for Department experiments	5,737.16
Coal, including all experiments	1,395.77
Salaries, etc	3,500.00
Insurance, sundries, etc	1,500.00
Total	21,746.93
Total value	34,476.50
Total cost	21,246.93
Net	13,229.57

Of the above labor bill, there has been paid—
By the Department	2,575.21
By the company	3,161.79

Of the above coal bill, there has been paid—
By the Department	324.00
By the company	1,071.77

Of the above cane account, there has been paid—
By the Department	324.00
By the company	9,290.00

Or, of the above expenditures the Department has paid $3,234.75. Bills are now pending for $3,300, making in all $6,534.75, reducing our total cost from $21,746.93 to $15,212.18, and leaving a profit from the season's work of $19,764.32. It will thus be seen that in the working of the crop, including cane for experimental purposes, the Department of Agriculture has paid or been charged with $6,534.75. This includes

* The amount of sugar branded was 234,607 pounds. The number of cells full of cane from which the juice was boiled for sugar was 2,501, according to the record of the sugar-boiler.—E. B. C.

the labor for the various experiments, the changing and erection of new machinery for the trial of the same, and the salaries and wages of most of the high-priced help, and which, in the practical operation of a factory, will not be required.

Respectfully submitted.

W. L. PARKINSON,
Manager.

FORT SCOTT, KANS., *October 23*, 1887.

OUTLINE OF THE PROCESSES OF SUGAR-MAKING.

As now developed, the processes of making sugar from sorghum are as follows:

First, The topped cane is delivered at the factory by the farmers who grow it.

Second, The cane is cut by a machine into pieces about 1¼ inches long.

Third, The leaves and sheaths are separated from the cut cane by fanning mills.

Fourth, The cleaned cane is cut into fine bits called chips.

Fifth, The chips are placed in iron tanks, and the sugar "diffused"—soaked out with hot water.

Sixth, The juice obtained by diffusion has its acids nearly or quite neutralized with milk of lime, and is heated and skimmed.

Seventh, The defecated or clarified juice is boiled to a semi-sirup in vacuum pans.

Eighth, The semi-sirup is boiled "to grain" in a high vacuum in the "strike-pan."

Ninth, The mixture of sugar and molasses from the strike-pan is passed through a mixing machine into centrifugal machines, which throw out the molasses and retain the sugar.

DETAILS OF THE PROCESSES OF SUGAR-MAKING.

An account of the processes of sugar-making ought doubtless to begin with the planting and cultivation, growth and ripening, of the cane, for it is here that the sugar is made. No known processes of science or art, save those of plant growth, produce the peculiar combination of carbon with the elements of water which we call sugar. Not only is this true, but the chemist utterly fails in every attempt to so modify existing similar combinations of these elements as to produce cane sugar. It will be interesting here to note three substances of nearly the same composition, viz: Starch, sucrose or cane sugar, and glucose or grape sugar. Their compositions are much alike, and may be stated as follows:

	Carbon.	Water.
Starch *	12	10
Cane sugar	12	11
Grape sugar	12	12

* The chemical formulas for these compounds are: Starch, $C_6H_{10}O_5$; cane sugar, $C_{12}H_{22}O_{11}$; grape sugar, $C_6H_{12}O_6$; in which C represents an equivalent of carbon, H of hydrogen, and O of oxygen, or H_2O an equivalent of water.

The chemist produces glucose, or grape sugar, from either starch or sugar by treatment with acid, but all attempts have failed to produce cane sugar from either starch or grape sugar.

THE FARMER THE REAL SUGAR-MAKER.

The farmer then, or perhaps more accurately the power which impels the plant to select and combine in proper form and proportions the three elements, carbon, hydrogen, and oxygen, is the real sugar-maker. All after processes are merely devices for separating the sugar from the other substances with which it grows.

HOW IS THE SUGAR FORMED IN THE CANE?

The process of the formation of sugar in the cane is not fully determined; but analyses of canes made at different stages of growth show that the sap of growing cane contains a soluble substance having a composition and giving reactions similar to starch. As maturity approaches, grape sugar is also found in the juice. A 'further advance towards maturity discloses cane sugar with the other substances, and at full maturity perfect canes contain much cane sugar and little grape sugar and starchy matter.

In sweet fruits the change from grape sugar to cane sugar does not take place, or takes place but sparingly. The grape sugar is very sweet, however.

INVERSION OR CHANGE OF CANE SUGAR INTO GRAPE SUGAR.

Cane sugar, called also sucrose or crystallizable sugar, when in dilute solution, is changed very readily into grape sugar or glucose, a substance which is much more difficult than cane sugar to crystallize. This change, called inversion, takes place in overripe canes; it sets in very soon after cutting in any cane during warm weather; it occurs in cane which has been injured by blowing down or by insects or by frost, and it probably occurs in cane which takes a second growth after nearly or quite reaching maturity.

Inversion will be further considered in another place.

THE FARMER'S PART MOST IMPORTANT OF ALL.

Since sugar is produced only by nature's processes of growth and is easily lost through inversion, it is evident that the farmer's part in the process of sugar-making is first and most important of all. It is a subject which invites most careful, scientific, and practical attention, and will be further considered under the subject "Improving the cane."

It is apparent from what has already been said, that to insure a successful outcome from the operations of the factory, the cane must be so planted, cultivated, and matured as to make the sugar in its juice;

that it must be delivered to the factory very soon after cutting; and that it must be taken care of before the season of heavy frosts.

THE WORK AT THE FACTORY.

THE FIRST CUTTING.

The operations of the factory are illustrated in the large drawing, to which the reader is referred in tracing the successive steps. The first cutting is accomplished in the ensilage or feed-cutter. This cutter is provided with three knives, fastened to the three spokes of a cast-iron wheel, which makes about 250 revolutions per minute, carrying the knives with a shearing motion past a dead knife. By a forced feed the cane is so fed as to be cut into pieces about 1¼ inches long. This cutting frees the leaves and nearly the entire sheaths from the pieces of cane. By a suitable elevator the pieces of cane, leaves, and sheaths are carried to the second floor.

THE CLEANING.

The elevator empties into a hopper, below which a series of four or five fans is arranged one below the other. By passing down through these fans the cane is separated from the lighter leaves much as grain is separated from chaff. The leaves are blown away, and finally taken from the building by an exhaust fan. This separation of the leaves and other refuse is essential to the success of the sugar-making, for in them the largest part of the coloring and other deleterious matters are contained. If carried into the diffusion battery these matters are extracted (see reports of Chemical Division, U. S. Department of Agriculture), and go into the juice with the sugar. As already stated, the process of manufacturing sugar is essentially one of separation. The mechanical elimination of these deleterious substances at the outset at once obviates the necessity of separating them later and by more difficult methods, and relieves the juice of their harmful influences. From the fans the pieces of cane are delivered by a screw carrier to an elevator, which discharges into

THE FINAL CUTTING-MACHINE.

on the third floor. This machine consists of an 8-inch cast-iron cylinder with knives like those of a planing-machine. It is really three cylinders placed end to end on the same shaft, making the entire length 18 inches. The knives are inserted in slots and held in place with set-screws. The cylinder revolves at the rate of about 1,200 per minute, carrying the knives past an iron dead knife, which is set so close that no cane can pass without being cut into fine chips. From this cutter the chips of cane are taken by an elevator and a conveyor to the cells of the diffusion battery. The conveyor passes above and at one side of the battery, and is provided with an opening and a spout opposite each cell of the battery. The openings are closed at pleasure by a slide. A movable spout completes the connection with any cell which it is desired to fill with chips.

WHAT IS DIFFUSION?

The condition in which the sugars and other soluble substances exist in the cane is that of solution in water. This sweetish liquid is contained, like the juices of plants generally, in cells. The walls of these cells are porous. It has long been known that if a solution of sugar in water be placed in a porous or membranous sack and the sack placed in water, an action called osmose takes place, whereby the water from the outside and the sugar solution from the inside of the sack each pass through until the liquids on the two sides of the membrane are equally sweet. Other substances soluble in water behave similarly, but sugar and other readily crystallizable substances pass through much more readily than uncrystallizable or difficultly crystallizable bodies. To apply this property to the extraction of sugar the cane is first cut into fine chips, as already described, and put into the diffusion cells, where water is applied and the sugar is displaced.

WHAT HAS TAKEN PLACE IN THE DIFFUSION CELLS.

For the purpose of illustration, let us assume that when a cell has been filled with chips just as much water is passed into the cell as there was juice in the chips. The process of osmose or diffusion sets in, and in a few minutes there is as much sugar in the liquid outside of the cane cells as in the juice in these cane cells; i. e., the water and the juice have divided the sugar, each taking half. Again, assume that as much liquid can be drawn from one as there was water added. It is plain that if the osmotic action is complete the liquid drawn off will be half as sweet as cane juice. It has now reached fresh chips in two, and again equalization takes place. Half of the sugar from one was brought into two, so that it now contains $1\frac{1}{2}$ portions of sugar, dissolved in 2 portions of liquid, or the liquid has risen to $\frac{3}{4}$ of the strength of cane juice. This liquid having $\frac{3}{4}$ strength passes to three, and we have in three $1\frac{3}{4}$ portions of liquid, or after the action has taken place the liquid in three is $\frac{7}{8}$ strength. One portion of this liquid passes to four, and we have $1\frac{7}{8}$ portions of sugar in 2 portions of liquid, or the liquid becomes $\frac{15}{16}$ strength. One portion of this liquid passes to five, and we have in five $1\frac{15}{16}$ portions of sugar in 2 portions of liquid, or the liquid is $\frac{31}{32}$ strength. It is now called *juice*, and is drawn off and subjected to the processes of the subsequent operations of the factory. From this time forward a cell is drawn for every one filled.

a	1	2	3	4	5	6	7	8	9	10	11	12
1	w											
2	w	l										
3	w	l	l									
4	w	l	l	l								
5	w	l	l	l	l							
6	w	l	l	l	l	l						
7	w	l	l	l	l	l	j					
8	w	l	l	l	l	l	l	j				
9	w	l	l	l	l	l	l	l	j			
10		w	l	l	l	l	l	l	l	j		
11	l		w	l	l	l	l	l	l	l	j	
12				w	l	l	l	l	l	l	l	j
13	j				w	l	l	l	l	l	l	l
14	l	j				w	l	l	l	l	l	l
15	l	l	j				w	l	l	l	l	l
16	l	l	l	j				w	l	l	l	l
17	l	l	l	l	j				w	l	l	l
18	l	l	l	l	l	j				w	l	l
19	l	l	l	l	l	l	j				w	l
20	l	l	l	l	l	l	l	j				w
21	w	l	l	l	l	l	l	l	j			
22		w	l	l	l	l	l	l	l	j		
23			w	l	l	l	l	l	l	l	j	
24				w	l	l	l	l	l	l	l	j
25	j				w	l	l	l	l	l	l	l
26	l	j				w	l	l	l	l	l	l
27	l	l	j				w	l	l	l	l	l
28	l	l	l	j				w	l	l	l	l
29	l	l	l	l	j				w	l	l	l

Throughout the operation the temperature is kept as near the boiling point as can be done conveniently without danger of filling some of the battery cells with steam. Diffusion takes place more rapidly at high than at low temperatures, and the danger of fermentation, with the consequent loss of sugar, is avoided. The process will be readily understood from the above diagram, in which the columns represent the cells of the battery, the numbers at the left the number of diffusions; *w*, water; *l*, liquid in the cells, or passing through them, and *j*, juice to be drawn.

INVERSION OF SUGAR IN THE DIFFUSION CELLS.

In the experiments at Fort Scott in 1886 much difficulty was experienced on account of inversion of the sugar in the diffusion battery. The report shows that this resulted from the use of soured cane and from delays in the operation of the battery on account of the imperfect working of the cutting and elevating machinery, much of which was then experimental. Under the circumstances, however, it became a matter of the gravest importance to find a method of preventing this inversion without in any manner interfering with the other processes. On the suggestion of Professor Swenson a portion of freshly precipitated carbonate of lime was placed with the chips in each cell. In the case of soured cane this took up the acid which otherwise produced inversion. In case no harmful acids were present this chalk was entirely inactive. Soured canes are not desirable to work under any circumstances, and should be rejected by the chemist and not allowed to enter the factory. So, also, delays on account of imperfect machinery are disastrous to profitable manufacturing and must be avoided. But for those who desire to experiment with deteriorated canes and untried cutting-machines, the addition of the calcium carbonate provides against disastrous results which would otherwise be inevitable.

CLARIFYING OR DEFECATING THE JUICE.

Immediately after it is drawn from the diffusion battery the juice is taken from the measuring tanks into the defecating tanks or pans. These are large, deep vessels, provided with copper steam coils in the bottom for the purpose of heating the juice. Sufficient milk of lime is added here to nearly or quite neutralize the acids in the juice, the test being made with litmus paper. The juice is brought to the boiling point, and as much of the scum is removed as can be taken quickly. The scum is returned to the diffusion cells, and the juice is sent by a pump to the top of the building, where it is boiled and thoroughly skimmed. These skimmings are also returned to the diffusion cells.

This method of disposing of the skimmings was suggested by Mr. Parkinson. It is better than the old plan of throwing them away to decompose and create a stench about the factory. Probably a better method would be to pass these skimmings through some sort of filter, or perhaps better still, to filter the juice and avoid all skimming. After this last skimming the juice is ready to be boiled down to a thin sirup, in

THE DOUBLE-EFFECT EVAPORATORS.

These consist of two large closed pans provided within with steam pipes of copper, whereby the liquid is heated. They are also connected with each other and with pumps in such a way as to reduce the pressure in the first to about three-fifths and in the second to about one-fifth the normal atmospheric pressure.

The juice boils rapidly in the first at somewhat below the temperature of boiling water, and in the second at a still lower temperature. The exhaust steam from the engines is used for heating the first pan, and the vapor from the boiling juice in the first pan is hot enough to do all the boiling in the second, and is taken into the copper pipes of the second for this purpose. In this way the evaporation is effected without so great expenditure of fuel as is necessary in open pans, or in single-effect vacuum pans, and the deleterious influences of long-continued high temperature on the crystallizing powers of the sugar are avoided.

From the double effects the sirup is stored in tanks ready to be taken into the strike-pan, where the sugar is crystallized.

THE FIRST CHANCE TO PAUSE.

At this point the juice has just reached a condition in which it will keep. From the moment the cane is cut in the fields until now every delay is liable to entail loss of sugar by inversion. After the water is put into the cells of the battery with the chips, the temperature is carefully kept above that at which fermentation takes place most readily, and the danger of inversion is thereby reduced. But with all the precautions known to science up to this point the utmost celerity is necessary to secure the best results. There is here, however, a natural division in the process of sugar-making, which will be further considered under the heading of "auxiliary factories." Any part of the process heretofore described may be learned in a few days by workmen of intelligence and observation who will give careful attention to their respective duties.

BOILING THE SIRUP TO GRAIN THE SUGAR.

This operation is the next in course, and is performed in what is known at the sugar factory as the strike-pan, a large air-tight vessel from which the air and vapor are almost exhausted by means of a suitable pump and condensing apparatus. As is the case with the saccharine juices of other plants, the sugar from sorghum crystallizes most readily at medium temperature. There are two ways of proceeding. The simplest is to boil the sirup in the vacuum pan until it has reached about the density at which crystallization begins, then draw it off into suitable vessels and set it away in a hot room (about 110° to 120° F.) to crystallize slowly. The proper density is usually judged by the boiler, by observing the length to which a sample of the hot liquid from the pan can be drawn. This is called the "string proof" test. A far better method is to "boil to grain" in the pan. This is better because it gives the operator control of the size of the grain within certain limits, because it gives a better appearing sugar, and more important still, because with proper skill it gives a better yield. Several descriptions of this delicate operation have been published. After reading some of the best of these, the writer found, on attempting to boil to grain, that more definite instruction was necessary; and after obtaining the instruction it became apparent that while almost any one can learn to "boil to grain," yet to obtain the best yield requires personal skill and powers of observation and comparison which will be obtained in widely different degrees by different persons. To become a good sugar-boiler, one must be an enthusiastic specialist. The Parkinson Sugar Company were fortunate in securing for this important work the services of Mr. Frederick Hinze, a native of Hanover, Germany, and a graduate of the "Sugar Industry School" at Braunschweig. Though a young man, Mr. Hinze has had a large experience, having assisted his brother in the erection and operation of sugar factories in Germany, and since coming to America having worked in the beet sugar factory at Alvarado, Cal., and in cane-sugar factories in Louisiana and in Cuba. Since the close of the working season at Fort Scott, Mr. Hinze has again gone to Louisiana and taken charge of a strike-pan at the sugar house of Ex-Governor Warmoth, where he worked last season.

The process of boiling to grain may be described as follows: A portion of the sirup is taken into the pan, and boiled rapidly *in vacuo* to the crystallizing density. If in a sirup the molecules of sugar are brought sufficiently near to each other through concentration—the removal of the dissolving liquid—these molecules attract each other so strongly as to overcome the separating power of the solvent, and they unite to form crystals. Sugar is much more soluble at high than at low temperatures, the heat acting in this as in almost all cases as a repulsive force among the molecules. It is therefore necessary to maintain a high vacuum in order to boil at a low pressure, in boiling to grain. When the proper density is reached, the crystals sometimes fail to appear, and a fresh portion of cold sirup is allowed to enter the pan. This must not be sufficient in amount to reduce the density of the contents of the pan below that at which crystallization may take place. This cold sirup causes a sudden though slight reduction of temperature, which may so reduce the repulsive forces as to allow the attraction among the molecules to prevail, resulting in the inception of crystallization. To discover this requires the keenest observation. When beginning to form, the crystals are too minute to show either form or size, even when viewed through a strong magnifying glass. There is to be seen simply a very delicate cloud. The inexperienced observer would entirely overlook this cloud, his attention probably being directed to some curious globular and annular objects, which I have nowhere seen explained. Very soon after the sample from the pan is placed upon glass for observation the surface becomes cooled and somewhat hardened. As the cooling proceeds below the surface contraction ensues, and consequently a wrinkling of the surface, causing a shimmer of the light in a very attractive manner. This, too, is likely to attract more attention than the delicate, thin cloud of crystals, and may be even confounded with the reflection and refraction of light, by which alone the minute crystals are determined. The practical operator learns to disregard all other attractions, and to look for the cloud and its peculiarities. When the contents of the pan have again reached the proper density another portion of sirup is added. The sugar which this contains is attracted to the crystals already formed, and goes to enlarge these rather than to form new crystals, provided the first are sufficiently numerous to receive the sugar as rapidly as it can crystallize.

The contents of the pan are repeatedly brought to the proper density, and fresh sirup added, as above described, until the desired size of grain is obtained, or until the pan is full. Good management should bring about these two conditions at the same time. If a sufficient number of crystals has not been started at the beginning of the operation to receive the sugar from the sirup added, a fresh crop of crystals will be started at such time as the crystallization becomes too rapid to be accommodated on the surfaces of the grain already formed. The older and larger crystals grow more rapidly, by reason of their greater attractive force, than the newer and smaller ones on succeeding additions of sirup, so that the disparity in size will increase as the work proceeds. This condition is by all means to be avoided, since it entails serious difficulties on the process of separating the sugar from the molasses. In case this second crop of crystals, called "false grain" or "mush sugar," has appeared, the sugar boiler must act upon his judgment, guided by his experience, as to what is to be done. He may take enough thin sirup into the pan to dissolve all of the crystals, and begin again, or, if very skillful, he may so force the growth of the false grain as to bring it up to a size that can be worked.

No attempt will be made here to describe the methods of "boiling for yield," nor to point out the methods by which many special difficulties are to be overcome. Not only does the limited experience of the writer make him hesitate to enter upon these intricate subjects, but their discussion would unduly extend this report. It may be remarked that the handling of the cane, the treatment of the juice, and the preparation of the sirup, have much to do with the difficulties and success of this the most intricate of all.

THE FINAL SEPARATION OF THE SUGAR FROM THE MOLASSES.

The completion of the work in the strike-pan leaves the sugar mixed with molasses. The mixture is called *melada* or *masse cuite*. It may be drawn off into iron sugar wagons and set in the hot room above mentioned, in which case still more of the sugar which remains in the uncrystallized state generally joins the crystals, somewhat increasing the yield of "first sugar." At the proper time these sugar wagons are emptied into a mixing machine, where the mass is brought to a uniform consistency. If the sugar wagons are not used, the strike-pan is emptied directly into the mixer.

THE CENTRIFUGAL MACHINES.

From the mixer the melada is drawn into the centrifugal machines. These consist, first, of an iron case resembling in form the husk of millstones. A spout at the bottom of the husk connects with a molasses tank. Within this husk is placed a metallic vessel with perforated sides. This vessel is either mounted or hung on a vertical axis, and is lined with wire cloth. Having taken a proper portion of the melada into the centrifugal, the operator starts it to revolving, and by means of a friction clutch makes such connection with the engine as gives it about 1,500 revolutions per minute. The centrifugal force developed drives the liquid molasses through the meshes of the wire cloth, and out against the husk, from which it flows off into a tank. The sugar, being solid, is retained by the wire cloth. If there is in the melada the "false grain" already mentioned, it passes into the meshes of the wire cloth, and prevents the passage of the molasses. After the molasses has been nearly all thrown out, a small quantity of water is sprayed over the sugar while the centrifugal is in motion. This is forced through the sugar, and carries with it much of the molasses which would otherwise adhere to the sugar, and discolor it. If the sugar is to be refined, this washing with water is omitted. When the sugar has been sufficiently dried, the machine is stopped, the sugar taken out, and put into barrels for market.

Simple as the operation of the centrifugals is, the direction of the sugar-boiler as to the special treatment of each strike is necessary, since he, better than any one else, knows what difficulties are to be expected on account of the condition in which the melada left the strike-pan.

CAPACITY OF THE SUGAR FACTORY.

It has already been shown that the operation of the diffusion battery should be continuous. The experience so far had in diffusing sorghum indicates eight minutes as the proper time for filling a cell; or one cell should be filled and another emptied every eight minutes. This, with a battery of twelve cells, nine of which are under pressure, gives seventy-two minutes as the time during which the chips are subject to the action of the water. If the chips are cut sufficiently fine, the time may be reduced to seven or even to six minutes to the cell without probable loss from poor extraction. The time may be extended to ten minutes per cell without danger of damage when working sound canes.

Taking eight minutes as the mean, we shall have one hundred and eighty as the number of cells diffused in a day. To secure the best results, all other parts of the factory must be adjusted to work as rapidly as the diffusion battery, so that the capacity of the battery will determine the capacity of the factory.

A plant having a battery like that at Fort Scott, in which the cells are each capable of containing a ton of cane chips, should then have a capacity of 180 tons of cleaned cane, or 200 tons of cane with leaves, or 240 tons of cane as it grows in the field, per day of twenty-four hours. Those who have given most attention to the subject think that a battery composed of 1½-ton cells may be operated quite as successfully as a battery of 1-ton cells. Such a battery would have a capacity of 360 tons of field cane per day.

SIMPLIFICATION OF THE DIFFUSION BATTERY.

The diffusion battery as used at the Parkinson factory is an intricate and expensive apparatus, and yet it is simple as compared with those first used in Germany and France. The Germans have, however, within a few years constructed batteries even simpler than that at Fort Scott. An apparatus has even been constructed composed of a single vessel through which the water passes in one direction while the chips are moved slowly in the other by a screw conveyor. The batteries which will be used in this country, however, will doubtless be constructed on the general plan of that used at Fort Scott, with such modifications as will cheapen the construction and reduce the labor of operating.

THE CUTTING AND CLEANING APPARATUS.

This consists of modifications of appliances which have long been used for other purposes. Simple as it is, and presenting only mechanical problems, the cutting, cleaning, and elevating apparatus is likely to be the source of more delays and perplexities in the operation of the sugar factory than any other part.

The diffusion battery in good hands works perfectly; the clarification of the juice causes no delays; the concentration to the condition of semi-sirup may be readily, rapidly, and surely effected in apparatus which has been brought to great perfection by long experience, and in many forms; the work at the strike-pan requires only to be placed in the hands of an expert; the mixer never fails to do its duty. There are various forms of centrifugal machines on the market, some of which are nearly perfect. If, then, the mechanical work of delivering, cutting, cleaning, and elevating the cane can be accomplished with regularity and rapidity, the operation of a well-adjusted sugar factory should proceed without interruption or delay from Monday morning to Saturday night.

The machines used at Fort Scott for these purposes have not been described in detail. They need only to be made stronger and simpler. Their general plan is not far from that which is likely to be in general use in the near future.

The methods of handling cane need some modifications as to details. The arrangement for making the factory engine unload the cane from the farmers' wagons will probably never be abandoned, since it is much more rapid and leaves the cane in better shape than it can be left by hand.

THE SCIENTIFIC WORK.

The present favorable condition of the sorghum-sugar industry, like the immense development of the beet-sugar industry of Europe, is indebted for its existence largely to long-continued scientific work; and while much of the scientific manipulation which it was once feared would be necessary to success has been eliminated in practice, yet the scientist has not been able to so far simplify the subject as to enable the manufacturer to dispense with his services. I shall try here to make a plain statement of the scientific work necessary in a sugar factory under developments so far made.

WHERE THE SCIENTIFIC WORK IS NEEDED.

It has already been shown that it is only on reaching maturity that sorghum is a profitable sugar plant. To determine when most farm products are ripe is a simple matter of inspection. But it is astonishing to note how greatly different will be the views of, say, a dozen practical farmers as to when a given field of wheat is ripe. Experience in judging of the ripeness of sorghum is far less extended than in the case of wheat. Indeed, the varying conditions of the weather so greatly affect the appearance of ripeness, *i. e.*, the hardness of the seed, the condition of the leaves, etc., that the manufacturer, who must know before he uses cane whether it is ripe or green, is left no other than the test of chemical analysis. This determines the one point of interest to him, namely, whether the cane has reached such a degree of maturity as to have made its sugar.

Again, although the cane may have reached full maturity, if it shall have been cut and exposed to the atmospheric influences of the earlier part of the season for any considerable time, the sugar may have been changed to glucose. In moist weather this change may take place without any accompanying change in the appearance of the cane. A notable instance illustrating this kind of depreciation occurred at the Parkinson works during the season just closed. A farmer brought in a sample of excellent-looking cane. The book-keeper, who has had considerable experience about sugar factories, examined it, and after ascertaining by the hydrometer that the juice contained about 13 per cent. of dissolved solids, was about to direct the farmer to bring in the cane. An analysis showed that about 8 of this 13 per cent. was glucose, 3 per cent. sugar, and 2 per cent. other substances not more valuable than glucose. Inquiry disclosed the fact that the cane had been cut for three days. The weather had been moist, so that no change in appearance had taken place. To have worked such cane for sugar would have been worse than useless, since the glucose and other substances its juice contained would have held from crystallization not only the 3 per cent. of sugar which this cane contained, but a considerable amount more had it been worked with better juice.

Instances might be multiplied to show the perplexities and disappointments which are liable to result unless a most careful supervision be had of the condition of the cane when it enters the factory. Certainly no field of cane should be cut until the development of its sugar has been reached and determined by the best means available.

In the early part of the season, while the weather is warm, all cane cut in the forenoon should be worked the same day, and that cut in the afternoon should be worked by noon the next day. During the cooler weather of the latter part of the season it is not necessary to be quite so prompt. The delays which will be admissible can be determined by analysis of the cane.

Not only is it necessary to know that the cane enters the factory with its sugar intact, but it is important to see that it does not suffer inversion during the process of manufacture. To prevent this all delays must be avoided. The cane must go promptly and regularly through the cutters and cleaners as rapidly as it can be thoroughly diffused. In a pile of cane chips inversion of the sugar very soon begins, and is soon followed, if not accompanied, by acetic fermentation. If acetic or other active acid be present in the diffusion cells it causes rapid inversion of the sugar under the high temperature of the battery. After leaving the battery the treatment of the juice must be prompt to guard against inversion. Indeed, as has been remarked above, every part of the factory in which the work is done until the juice has been reduced to a sirup should be of such a capacity that it can surely do its work at all times as rapidly as the battery can be operated. It is a matter of great importance to the manufacturer to know whether, at any stage of the process, inversion is taking place. To determine this the analysis of average samples of freshly-cut chips may be compared with analysis of the product at other stages. For example: To determine whether inversion is taking place in the battery, crush out and analyze the juice from samples of chips as they enter; then analyze samples of the diffu. sion juice as it comes from the battery. If the relation of sugar to glucose is the same in these analyses it may be concluded that no inversion is taking place. If, however, the proportion of sugar to glucose is smaller in the diffusion juice than in that obtained directly from the chips by crushing, inversion is probably taking place, and its cause must be sought and remedied.

The subsequent processes of manufacture give little occasion for inversion, unless from delay before the juice has been reduced to sirup. The safest plan is to not let it cool until it is ready for the strike-pan. If unavoidable delays lead to a suspicion that inversion may have taken place, the matter may be determined by analysis. Inversion is not the only cause of loss to be guarded against in the battery. As shown by the report of the chemist of the United States Department of Agriculture, the average extraction of the battery at the Parkinson factory this season was 92.04 per cent. of all the sugars the cane contained. A closer average extraction than 95 per cent. is scarcely to be expected, and an extraction of less than 90 per cent. should be considered inadmissible. Poor extraction may result from overhurrying the battery, from allowing the temperature to run too low, from raising the temperature too highly, thereby filling the upper parts of the cells with steam instead of water, or from improper manipulation of the valves, or from failure of the cutting machines to properly prepare the chips. The perfection of the extraction may be determined by analysis of the exhausted chips from the battery, and if not found satisfactory, the cause is of course to be sought out and remedied.

It is desirable for the manufacturer to know how much sugar he is leaving in the molasses, and also how much molasses he is leaving in the sugar; i. e., the purity of the sugar. These points are readily determined by analysis.

WHO CAN DO THIS SCIENTIFIC WORK?

It is doubtless desirable, though not essential, that the superintendent of a sugar factory be also a chemist. The analyses indicated in the above pages are not intricate. To make them all, however, will require considerable time, and whether the superintendent be capable or incapable of making them, he will scarcely be able to spare the time which ought to be devoted to them.

Any of the graduates of our agricultural or other colleges who have taken a good course of chemistry, with laboratory practice, can by a few months' special training in sugar chemistry and practice in sugar analysis become entirely competent to do the work required in the ordinary operation of a factory, under the direction of the superintendent.

HOW TO MAKE THE ANALYSES NECESSARY IN THE SUGAR FACTORY.

It is hoped that the following discussion of the methods of making sugar analyses will be of interest to some who may engage in such work, and throw some light on the subject for the general reader. For fuller discussions of the subject, the reader is referred to Tucker's Sugar Analysis, and the bulletins of the Chemical Division, U. S. Department of Agriculture.

It is well to remember here, that on account of the sugar and other substances dissolved in it cane juice is denser than water. Thus, if 9 pounds of water and 1 pound of sugar be mixed together the water will dissolve the sugar, and any given volume of the mixture, say a pint, will weigh one and four-hundredths times as much as a pint of water. Take another illustration: A gallon of water weighs about 8⅓ pounds, while a gallon of the above supposed sugar solution weighs about 8⅔ pounds. If a sugar solution be made, containing 20 per cent. of its weight in sugar, a gallon of it will weigh about 9 pounds. A gallon of a solution of equal parts by weight of sugar and water weighs about 10¼ pounds, and sirups containing three parts sugar to one of water weigh about 11½ pounds to the gallon.

THE HYDROMETER OR SACCHARIMETER.

Instruments called hydrometers or saccharimeters have been made for determining the relative amounts of sugar and water in solutions. These would be sufficiently accurate for the purposes of the manufacturer if the juice contained nothing but cane sugar and water; but the grape sugar and other substances contained in the juice increase the density in about the same proportion as it is increased by the cane sugar. While, therefore, the hydrometer is of use in determining the amount of solid matter contained in the juice, and may be used in some cases, as in determining the degree of extraction, etc., it does not determine the relative proportions of the substances present.

TWO METHODS OF ANALYSIS.

Two methods of determining the percentage of cane sugar in a sample of juice are available. These are the chemical and the optical. By the first may be determined the percentages of, first, cane sugar; second, grape sugar, otherwise called glucose; third, "not sugar;" fourth, water; constituting the juice. By the second method, the cane sugar alone is determined. The optical method is, however, conveniently used in connection with the chemical, in making complete analyses. One of the chemical methods will be considered first. I shall go as little as possible into technicality·here.

FEHLING'S SOLUTION OF COPPER.

This is the principal reagent used in the chemical methods of analysis. There are several modifications of it. Perhaps none of these is better than *Violette's solution :* *

34.64 grams pure crystallized copper sulphate.

184.00 grams tartrate soda and potash (Rochelle salt).

78.00 grams caustic soda.

The copper salt is to be dissolved in 140 cubic centimeters of distilled water, slowly added to a solution of the tartrate and caustic soda, and the .whole made up to 1 liter at standard temperature ($17\frac{1}{2}°$ Centigrade; $63\frac{1}{2}°$ Fahrenheit). This should be a clear blue solution.

THE GRAPE-SUGAR TEST.

If now a portion of this copper solution be brought to a boil, and to it be added a solution containing grape sugar, the blue color will be changed through various shades of purple to crimson, and finally to scarlet. The reaction has reached the decisive stage when the color is crimson. On standing, the crimson precipitate settles to the bottom of the vessel. This is the reaction for the determination of grape sugar. If a definite quantity, say 10 cc., of the copper solution be used in the above experiment, a definite quantity of grape sugar, .05 grams, will have to be added to perfect the reaction. Now by noting the amount of sample added to complete the reaction, the determination of the percentage of grape sugar from the experimental data becomes a mere matter of arithmetic. Thus, if 4 grams of the sample had been added to produce the complete reaction, we should have known that those 4 grams of sample contained five-hundredths of a gram of grape sugar. .05÷4=.0125, or $1\frac{1}{4}$ per cent. of grape sugar.

THE CANE SUGAR TEST.

Cane sugar has no such effect on the copper solution. It has been remarked already that cane sugar changes very readily into grape sugar. This change is easily produced by boiling the solution of cane sugar; for example, the cane juice with dilute hydrochloric or sulphuric acid. The cane juice will now contain the grape sugar it originally con-

---

* Tucker's Sugar Analysis, p. 186.

tained, and in addition that which resulted from the inversion of the cane sugar. It now only remains to nearly neutralize the acid in the solution, cool it, and execute the test and calculations for grape sugar as before. Subtracting the percentage of grape sugar originally found from that shown by the last determination gives the percentage of grape sugar resulting from the inversion of the cane sugar. The percentage of cane sugar is .95 of the grape sugar produced by inversion of the cane sugar. The soluble solids "not sugar" contained in the juice may be estimated by subtracting the sum of the percentages of the two sugars from the entire percentage of soluble solids as determined by the hydrometer.

THE OPTICAL METHOD.

The optical method of determining the percentage of cane sugar depends upon the fact that a beam of polarized light is rotated to the right in passing through a solution of this sugar. While the apparatus for executing this test is expensive and the explanation intricate, the manipulation is simple and rapid and the results satisfactory; so that it is probable that all well-regulated sugar factories will be provided with these instruments.

For many of the purposes of the factory the determinations of the percentage of cane sugar is all that is required. The analyst will probably be able to make forty or fifty of these determinations per day by the optical method, if so many are required.

THE FURTHER SCIENTIFIC WORK.

The money, skill, and knowledge which have during the last few years been expended upon the sorghum plant have made available a new industry. The possibilities of this new industry can be fully understood only on more fully considering some of the facts which chemical science has made known.

The analyses made at the Parkinson Sugar Works during the season of 1887 by Dr. C. A. Crampton and Mr. Norman J. Fake, chemists of the U. S. Department of Agriculture, are of great value in this connection, and when supplemented by the further work now in progress in the laboratories of the Department at Washington will become a basis for future work.

In tables of analyses the percentages given are usually computed on the weight of the juice contained in the cane. Those who are familiar with the habit of the plant will readily see that the cane may be considered in three parts, viz: (1) The tops, including the seed and 12 to 18 inches of the upper part of the stalk; (2) the leaves, including the leaf sheaths; (3) the body of the cane after the tops and leaves have been removed. This body of the cane contains nearly all of the juice, and practically all of the sugar,

A ton of sorghum as it grows is composed of these three parts in about the following average proportions :

Topped and cleaned cane..pounds.. 1,500
Tops...do.... 300
Leaves and sheaths...do.... 200

Total...~.................... 2,000

The juice constitutes about 90 per cent. of the topped and cleaned cane. Analytical estimates and the estimates of the sugar factory are based on the ton of topped and cleaned cane. In order to place the matter clearly before the reader, and at the same time to compare the amount of sugar contained in Louisiana cane with that contained in sorghum, and to make other studies of the subject, I have computed from the analytical tables of the United States Department of Agriculture the weights of " cane sugar," " grape sugar," and soluble solids " not sugar," found to exist in the ton of topped and cleaned sorghum for the years 1883–'87, and in the ton of cleaned Louisiana cane for the years 1884–'86.

" Cane sugar," "grape sugar," and soluble solids " not sugar" contained in a ton of cleaned sorghum and cleaned Louisiana cane.

[Computed from the analytical tables of the United States Department of Agriculture, the weight of juice being assumed at 1,800 pounds per ton in either cane.]

Constituents.	1883.		1884.		1885.		1886.		1887.		Means.	
	Sorghum.	Louisiana cane.*	Sorghum.†	Louisiana cane.	Sorghum.	Louisiana cane.	Sorghum.	Louisiana cane.	Sorghum.	Louisiana cane.*	Sorghum.	Louisiana cane.
	Lbs.	Lbs.	Lbs.	Lbs.	Lbs.	Lbs.	Lbs.	Lbs.	Lbs.	Lbs.	Lbs.	Lbs.
Cane sugar	162.70		264.90	227.00	177.48	220.00	188.82	243.00	171.80		193.10	230.00
Grape sugar	73.44		22.32	15.66	50.00	18.00	62.00	11.00	60.00		53.55	14.89
Total sugars	236.14		287.22	242.66	227.48	238.00	250.82	254.00	231.80		246.65	244.89
Not sugar	30.42		64.44	47.88	50.00	44.00	53.00	37.60	50.00		49.97	43.16
Total soluble solids	266.56		361.64	290.54	277.48	282.00	303.82	291.60	281.80		296.62	288.05

* No record.
† The writer made a series of analyses of canes grown near Sterling, Kans., in 1884, taking the juice as it came from the crusher in the regular course of manufacture. The mean of these from the first mill gave 222 12 pounds of sugar per ton of cane. In his report of the crop of 1884 Dr. Wiley says the land on which the cane analyzed by him and included in the above summary was grown had a top-dressing of about 400 pounds of superphosphate per acre.

IMPROVING THE SEED.

The study of this table is most interesting. The first and most important observation is of the wide differences in the sorghum canes examined, there being a variation of 102.2 pounds of cane sugar per ton from 1883 to 1884. Every practical sugar-maker knows that the difference in the available sugar is greater than the actual difference shown in these analyses. Again, the cane sugar contained in the sorghum of 1884 exceeded that in the Louisiana cane of any year of the record.

If a naturalist were seeking a plant whose record indicated that it would yield readily to the influences of cultivation, a plant which might be changed in its characteristics, he would select one showing just such extreme variations as this. It is doubtless necessary only to reproduce the conditions, whatever they may have been, under which the crop of 1884 was produced to reproduce like results. These conditions may be no more difficult to attain than those which produce the average crop. This branch of the subject invites study and experiment. The opportunity doubtless exists to build up the sugar-producing properties of sorghum-making improvements not inferior to those by which the Europeans have made the sugar-beet a most valuable source of sugar.

In this connection, I can do no better than to produce and second the remarks of Dr. Wiley, in his report for 1883, on Improvement by Seed Selection.

I am fully convinced that the Government should undertake the experiments which have in view the increase of the ratio of sucrose to other substances in the juice. These experiments, to be valuable, must continue under proper scientific direction for a number of years. The cost will be so great that a private citizen will hardly be willing to undertake the expense.

The history of the improvement in the sugar beet should be sufficient to encourage all similar efforts with sorghum.

The original forage beet, from which the sugar beet has been developed, contained only 5 or 6 per cent. of sucrose. The sugar beet now will average 10 per cent. of sucrose. It seems to me that a few years of careful selection may secure a similar improvement in sorghum.

It would be a long step toward the solution of the problem to secure a sorghum that would average, field for field, 12 per cent. sucrose and only 2 per cent. of other sugars, and with such cane the great difficulty would be to make sirup and not sugar. Those varieties and individuals of each variety of cane which show the best analytical results should be carefully selected for seed, and this selection continued until accidental variations become hereditary qualities in harmony with the well-known principles of descent.

If these experiments in selection could be made in different parts of the country, and especially by the various agricultural stations and colleges, they would have additional value and force. In a country whose soil and climate are as diversified as in this, results obtained in one locality are not always reliable for another.

If some unity of action could in this way be established among those engaged in agricultural research, much time and labor would be saved and more valuable results be obtained.

A VALUABLE CONTENT OF SORGHUM CANE.

The grape-sugar content of sorghum is very large. When freed from such of the "not sugar" products as have an unpleasant taste, this constitutes an elegant sirup constituent. It is composed chiefly of two sugars, called, respectively, dextrose and levulose. The last is sweeter than cane sugar. This grape sugar is that to which most sweet fruits owe their sweetness. The large amount of it—over 53 pounds to the ton of cane—is likely to be recognized in the near future as one of the most valuable contents of sorghum cane.

IMPERFECT SEPARATION.

At present we are able to separate only a portion of the cane sugar from the other constituents of the juice. It is believed to be impossible by methods at present used to separate more than the difference between the cane sugar and the grape sugar. Thus the sorghum of 1883 could have yielded not more than $162.7 - 73.44 = 89.26$ pounds per ton, while that of 1884 should, by the same computation have yielded $264.9 - 22.32 = 242.58$ pounds per ton. The available sugar in the sorghum crop of 1887, by the same method, was $171.8 - 60 = 111.8$ pounds, and the average available sugar in the sorghum for the five years was $193.1 - 53.55 = 139.55$ pounds. This is supposing that the juice is all obtained from the cane, and that there is no waste in the subsequent processes. At Fort Scott, however, only a little more than 92 per cent. of the sugar was obtained from the cane, so that the above figures should be multiplied by .92, making the mean available sugar with this extraction 128.38 pounds, and the available sugar of 1887, 102.8 pounds per ton of cleaned cane.

THE YIELD OBTAINED AT FORT SCOTT.

The actual yield obtained was 234,607 pounds of first sugar, from 2,501 cells. If, now, the cell be taken as a ton, the yield of first sugar was $234,607 \div 2,501 = 93.8$ pounds. Enough of the molasses was reboiled for a second crop of crystals, and the sugar separated to ascertain that 15 to 20 pounds, per ton of cane represented, could be obtained. Calling it 15, we have for the entire yield $93.8 + 15 = 108.8$ pounds per ton of cleaned cane. This is a larger yield than is obtainable according to the heretofore accepted theory. There is some uncertainty about the weight of a cell, which may account for the discrepancy between the theoretical and the actual results. It is possible, however, that the theory may need reconstruction. In any case the yield actually obtained is most gratifying.

I have made no mention in the above of the exceptionally large yields of some special strikes made during the season. One strike gave 109 pounds of merchantable sugar for each cellful of chips. The seconds from this would doubtless have brought the yield up to 130 pounds. But the general reader and the prospective manufacturer are more interested in average than in special results. It seems safe to assume that a mean of 100 pounds of sugar and 12 gallons of molasses can be made from each ton of cleaned sorghum cane of average richness.

Science suggests several methods for the complete separation of the cane sugar from the grape sugar and the " not sugar," and further experiments in this direction should be the work of the near future. As yet almost nothing has been done towards the development of methods of separating the grape sugar from the not sugar. This subject presents a most inviting field for the chemist.

THE FUTURE OF THE SORGHUM-SUGAR INDUSTRY.

The sorghum-sugar industry now seems to have an assured future. The quantities of sugar and molasses, and other valuable products obtained from each ton of the cane and from each acre of land, well remunerate the farmer for his crop and the manufacturer for his investment and the labor and skill required to operate the factory.

An acre of land cultivated in sorghum yields a greater tonnage of valuable products than in any other crop, with the possible exception of hay. Under ordinary methods of cultivation, 10 tons of cleaned cane per acre is somewhat above the average, but the larger varieties often exceed 12, while the small Early Amber sometimes goes below 8 tons per acre. Let 7½ tons of cleaned cane per acre be assumed for the illustration. This corresponds to a gross yield of 10 tons for the farmer, and at $2 per ton gives him $20 per acre for his crop. These 7½ tons of clean cane will yield—

	Pounds.
Sugar	750
Molasses	1,000
Seed	900
Fodder (green leaves)	1,500
Exhausted chips (dried)	1,500
Total	5,650

The first three items, which are as likely to be transported as wheat or corn, aggregate 2,650 pounds per acre.

Sorghum will yield 7½ tons of cleaned cane per acre more surely than corn will yield 30 bushels, or wheat 15 bushels per acre.

In the comparison, then, of products which bear transportation, these crops stand as follows:

Sorghum, at 7½ tons, 2,650 pounds per acre.
Corn, at 30 bushels, 1,680 pounds per acre.
Wheat, at 15 bushels, 900 pounds per acre.

The sugar from the sorghum is worth say 5 cents per pound; the molasses, 1¾ cents per pound; the seed, ½ cent per pound.

The products give market values as follows:

750 pounds sugar at say 5 cents*	$37.50
1,000 pounds molasses at say 1¾ cents*	17.50
900 pounds seed at say ½ cent*	4.50
Total value of sorghum, less fodder	59.50
The corn crop gives 1,680 pounds, at ½ cent	8.40
The wheat crop gives 900 pounds, at 1 cent	9.00

Thus it will be seen that the sorghum yields to the farmer more than twice as much per acre as either of the leading cereals, and as a gross

* The sugar sold this year at 5¼ cents per pound, the molasses at 20 cents per gallon, and the seed at —— per bushel of 56 pounds. The seed is of about equal value with corn for feeding stock.

product of agriculture and manufacture on our own soil more than six times as much per acre as is usually realized from either of these standard crops.

LENGTH OF THE SEASON FOR WORKING SORGHUM.

The season for harvesting sorghum is limited to the months during which it may be worked. At present, this dates in our southern counties from about the last of July to the middle or last of October, if a proper selection of varieties of cane has been made. Without doubt this season may, and will be, lengthened. On this point I can do no better than quote from my report to this Department in 1884:

As shown by the reports of the sugar factories of Kansas for the last two years, the working season is confined almost exclusively to the months of September and October. When the great cost of sugar-works, the expense of keeping them in repair, and the salaries of the specialists, are considered, the importance of lengthening the working season becomes painfully apparent. That a $100,000 factory should lie idle for ten months every year, implies that it must be run at an enormous profit during the two months or fail to pay interest on the investment.

Several plans have been proposed for extending the time during which the works may run. One of these is the development of earlier varieties of cane by systematic selection of seed, cultivation, and breeding. The researches of modern physiological botanists give reason to hope for good results in this direction.

Another plan proposed is to reduce the juice to a semi-sirup in small auxiliary factories, store the semi-sirup, and make it into sugar during the winter months. This has much to commend it.

STORING CANES IN SILOS.

Experiments have been made repeatedly in keeping canes in sheds, but with indifferent success. A good deal has been done in the line of preserving green forage crops in pits, and expensive silos have been made and used. Sorghum has been laid away and kept in these with fair success.

A practical plan for keeping cane by simply covering it with a few inches of soil has been used in three experiments now on record. The first of these was made at Tilsonburg, Ontario, in 1831–'82, by Mr. Frank Stroback, now of Sterling, Kans. Mr. Stroback has kindly handed me a copy of his record, which is given below, with the addition of the column giving the density of the juice in degrees Baumé, to render these results more easily comparable with the other analyses given in this paper.

Frank Stroback's experiment in keeping cane in silo.

When put in silo.	Baumé.	Balling.	Polarization.
October 3, 1881	8. 20 to 8. 80°	14. 00 to 15. 00°	....
December 3, 1881	8. 15	14. 70	12. 28
December 17, 1882	7. 70	13. 90	9. 82
March 4, 1882	7. 55	13. 61	9. 07

The cane used in this experiment was the early amber. The juice showed a depreciation, but the results were encouraging.

In the fall of 1883, Professor Wiley, chief chemist of the U. S. Department of Agriculture, placed a ton of early amber in a shallow pit, and placed over it a covering of earth on the grounds of the Department of Agriculture at Washington. In his report of April 22, 1884, Professor Wiley gives an account of this experiment, from which the following information is taken :

The canes were placed in silo November 12, 1883. Numerous analyses of juices of canes similar to those preserved showed—

Sucrose, about 9 per cent.

Other sugars, about 3 per cent.

Professor Wiley's analysis of cane from silo, January 14, 1884.

Percentage of juice expressed... 68.9
Specific gravity, 8° B 1.057
Percentage of sucrose.. 8.39
Percentage of other sugars... 2.36

Analysis of cane from silo, February 27, 1884.

Percentage of juice expressed... 73.67
Specific gravity... 1.057
Percentage of sucrose.. 7.00
Percentage of other sugars 3.13

Analysis of cane from silo, April 1, 1884.

Percentage of juice expressed... 73.81
Specific gravity... 1.05
Percentage of sucrose.. 5.89
Percentage of other sugars 3.72

I was greatly interested in these results, which showed that the early amber cane can be kept during the greater part of the winter with very little depreciation of its content of sugar.

In order to extend the experiment to other varieties, and to test the possibility of keeping Kansas canes in silo, on October 15, 1884, I placed 1 ton of Link's hybrid and 1 ton of early orange in winrows between rows of stubble, and placed thereon a covering of about 2 inches of sandy soil. Analyses were made on the day on which they were buried, and subsequently, as shown in the following tables:

Analyses of juices of canes kept in silo.

Date.	Remarks.	B.	Glucose.	Sucrose.	Other solids.
	EARLY ORANGE.				
1884.	(Produced by J. B. Keeley, 2 miles southwest from Sterling.)				
Oct: 15	Cut yesterday afternoon, buried to-day......	11.8	.95	15.62	4.73
Nov. 15	Leaves molded, canes green—interior of canes reddened to first node, top and bottom	10.8	4.88	10.72	3.90
Nov. 29	Appearance unchanged since 15th instant	10.7	4.03	9.45	5.82
Dec. 26	Appearance unchanged since November	9.8	1.19	11.69	4.82
1885.					
Jan. 24	186 pounds cane gave 100 pounds juice = 53¾ per cent. on hand-crusher..	11.2	4.80	10.85	4.55
	LINK'S HYBRID.				
1884.					
Oct. 15	Cut and buried to-day	9.8	1.16	11.21	5.33
Nov. 15	Leaves molded, canes green—interior of canes reddened to first node, top and bottom	10.2	1.11	13.02	4.37
Nov. 29	Appearance unchanged since 15th instant	10.3	1.49	12.26	4.83
Dec. 26	Some of the canes show decomposition where they had been bruised	10.7	2.72	12.93	3.65
1885.					
Jan. 29	Small sample analyzed	11.0	5.49	11.40	2.91
Jan. 30	600 pounds cane gave 312 pounds juice = 52 per cent. on hand-crusher; defecated by adding milk of lime, boiling and skimming	11.5	5.35	11.22	4.23
Feb. 2	Above boiled to 17° B., hot, in open-fire pan	25.0	11.49	24.10	10.21

Samples of the canes taken from the silo on the 26th of December were sent to Professor Swenson, superintendent of the Hutchinson Sugar Works. On the 4th of January, 1885, Professor Swenson reported the following as the results of his examination of the Link's Hybrid cane:

JUICE.

	Per cent.
Sucrose	15.25
Glucose	1.10
Other solids	3.94

ENTIRE CANE.

Insoluble solids	11.72
Sucrose	13.73
Glucose	1.00
Other soluble solids	2.25
Water	71.00
Total	100.00

Mr. J. C. Hart, superintendent of the farm of the Hutchinson Sugar Works, reported the following results of examinations of the Early Orange cane taken from the silo December 26:

Analysis of January 5, sucrose and glucose taken from diffusion juice.

	Per cent.
Water	67.7
Insolubles	13.9
Sucrose	14.8
Glucose	1.6
Gums, etc	2.0
Total	100.0

Analysis of January 7, from expressed juice.

Sucrose	14.0
Glucose	3.2
Gum, etc	4.8

On the 9th of January canes were again taken from the silo and submitted to Prof. M. A. Scovell, superintendent of the Sterling works, for analysis. The following results are taken from his report:

LINK'S HYBRID.

Amount of canes taken	pounds..	18
Amount of juice expressed	do....	7¼
Juice	per cent..	41¾
Density of juice, 10.6 B.		
Glucose	per cent..	5.53
Sucrose	do....	9.73

ORANGE.

Amount of canes taken	pounds..	12
Amount of juice, 4 pounds	per cent..	33¼
Density of juice, 10.7 B.		
Glucose	per cent..	5.83
Sucrose	do....	8.84

Samples of the canes taken from the silo on January 9 were sent to the Hutchinson Sugar Works, to the State Agricultural college, and to the State University for analysis.

On January 12, Mr. J. C. Hart, of the Hutchinson works, reported the following average of two analyses, crushed juice.

	Orange cane. Brix, 22°.	Link's Hybrid cane. Brix, 21.7°.
	Per cent.	Per cent.
Water	69.90	68.20
Insoluble solids	10.50	12.90
Glucose	3.45	3.20
Sucrose	12.34	12.19
Other solids	3.81	3.51
	100.00	100.00

Prof. G. H. Fallyer, professor of chemistry in the State Agricultural college, made the following report of his analyses of these canes on January 14:

	Orange cane.	Link's Hybrid cane.
Percentage of juice	44.0	45.5
Specific gravity	1.0876	1.0809
Sucrose, per cent	9.82	9.06
Glucose, per cent	0.84	6.65

Summarizing the results of these analyses as to cane sugar, we find that they stand as follows:

Date.	Variety of cane.	Variety of cane.	Name of analyst.
Oct. 15	Link's Hybrid, 11.21 per cent. sugar	Orange, 15.62 per cent. sugar	Cowgill.
Nov. 15	Link's Hybrid, 13.02 per cent. sugar	Orange, 10.72 per cent. sugar	Cowgill.
Nov. 29	Link's Hybrid, 12.26 per cent. sugar	Orange, 9.45 per cent. sugar	Cowgill.
Dec. 26	Link's Hybrid, 12.93 per cent. sugar	Orange, 11.69 per cent. sugar	Cowgill.
Jan. 4	Link's Hybrid, 15.25 per cent. sugar		Swenson.
Jan. 5		Orange, 14.8 per cent. sugar	Hart.
Jan. 7		Orange, 14.0 per cent. sugar	Hart.
Jan. 9	Link's Hybrid, 9.73 per cent sugar	Orange, 8.84 per cent. sugar	Scovell.
Jan. 12	Link's Hybrid, 12.19 per cent. sugar	Orange, 12.34 per cent. sugar	Hart.
Jan. 14	Link's Hybrid, 9.06 per cent. sugar	Orange, 9.82 per cent. sugar	Fallyer.
Jan. 24		Orange, 10.85 per cent. sugar	Cowgill.
Jan. 29	Link's Hybrid, 11.40 per cent. sugar		Cowgill.

It should be remarked that the samples taken from the silo, January 9, were those which had been most exposed to the action of the sun and wind on account of the frequent opening of the silo. This may account for the great depreciation shown by the analysis of these samples.

The juice obtained on January 24 from the Early Orange cane was defecated with milk of lime, boiled, skimmed, and settled, and reduced to semi-sirup, 17° B., hot, in the usual way in open fire pan. It was then taken into a small vacuum pan and boiled to nearly the crystallizing point by Mr. Frank Stroback, an experienced sugar-boiler. It was then drawn off and set away in a warm place, and is crystallizing into a fine melada.

The juice obtained on January 29 from the Link's Hybrid cane was treated in a manner precisely similar to that above described for the Early Orange, except that it was "boiled to grain" in the vacuum pan by Mr. Stroback. This was effected as follows: Ten quarts of semi-sirup were first introduced, and boiled *in vacuo* to the crystallizing density. A pint of cold semi-sirup was then added, and the contents of the pan again reduced to the crystallizing density. The process of adding a pint of semi-sirup and reducing to the crystallizing density was repeated until the boiling was complete. After a few of these additions had been made, a slight turbidity of the sirup was observed. On placing the sirup now under a microscope and examining it by transmitted light, the turbidity was seen to result from countless microscopic crystals of sugar. The subsequent additions of semi-sirup fed these minute crystals, and they continued to grow in size as long as the operation was continued.

It is well known to sugar-boilers that it is impossible to crystallize in the pan the sugar from very poor juices. The success, therefore, of this last experiment abundantly verifies the results of the chemical analysis, which showed that this Link's Hybrid cane contained on the 29th of January very nearly the same percentage of sugar as when put away on the 15th of October. Mr. Stroback states that the crystallization was as easily produced as at any time during the working season of 1884.

It is therefore fully established that some varieties of sorghum cane can be preserved in an inexpensive way without impairment of the sugar until the last of January. It is desirable that the experiment be extended to other of the late varieties, notably the Honduras, which yields 15 tons to 30 tons per acre, but does not perfect its sugar during the regular fall working season.

CENTRAL AND AUXILIARY FACTORIES—SIZE OF FACTORIES.

The complete sugar factory is an expensive establishment, and while most of the work of operating it can be performed by laboring men of ordinary intelligence, there will be required in each of such factories, whether large or small, at least two men whose attainments will command liberal compensation. These are the chemist, or the superintendent with a cheaper chemist for an assistant, and the sugar-boiler. Good business management is of course also necessary to success. The chemist and the sugar-boiler can preside over a large as well as over a small factory. Moreover, many of the labors of the factory can be performed with no fewer men in a small than in a large factory. It will therefore be cheaper to work a given amount of cane and to turn out a given amount of product in large than in small factories. The limit, however, beyond which experience so far does not warrant manufacturers to go is believed to be at a capacity of about 270 tons of cleaned cane per day.

In order to use to the best advantage the services of the specialists of the business, it has been proposed to establish at convenient places auxiliary factories which shall carry the processes so far as to prepare sirup for the strike-pan. This sirup will be stored in suitable tanks or cisterns and worked for sugar after the close of the season for handling cane. In this way the working season for the central factory may be prolonged to occupy almost the entire year. The auxiliary factories will cost about half or two-thirds as much as the complete factory, capable of taking care of the same amount of cane. As thus arranged, the central factory will, in addition to its own regular season's work, take care of the sirup from two or three of these sirup factories.

It will doubtless be found economical to provide the central factory with sugar apparatus of two or three times the capacity required to take care of its own sirup, thereby increasing the number of auxiliaries which may be made dependent upon it. It must not be inferred from what is here said that the sugar factory can make sugar from ordinary sorghum molasses. The auxiliaries will necessarily be under the supervision of the central factory, and the value of its sirups will depend upon the proper execution of the processes of manufacture. The sirups from the auxiliaries may be transported to the central factory in tank cars or by pipe lines.

HOW FAR MAY CANE BE HAULED?

The price paid for cane delivered at the sugar factory has heretofore been $2 per ton. It needs only to be stated that long hauls by wagon would cost too much to leave any profit to the farmer at this price. It is doubtful whether the farmer who lives more than 3 miles from the factory can afford to raise cane unless he can transport it most of the way by rail. Again, the factory will easily obtain all it can work from farmers whose distance does not exceed 2 miles, and will prefer to patronize these on account of the greater regularity with which they can deliver their crops, as well as the greater facility with which the supervision of the factory may be extended. Farmers living on a line of railroad may be able to ship their cane on such favorable terms as to avail themselves of the market at the factory. In Cuba and in some parts of Louisiana, light railroads are constructed where the distance is too great for hauling on ordinary roads. On these a team hauls about 13 tons at a load.

The system of central and auxiliary factories seems, however, to offer the best solution for the problem of distance.

CAN THE FARMER MAKE HIS OWN SUGAR FROM SORGHUM?

Several experimenters have sought to answer this question in a practical way. The developments of the last few years have clearly established the fact that the cane-crusher has had its day. Hereafter the juice will be extracted by the process of diffusion, whereby at least double the yield possible with crushers is obtained, at the same time giving a juice which may be readily treated.

Mr. H. A. Hughes, of Rio Grande, N. J., has been experimenting with a small diffusion battery, and has this season worked 80 acres of sorghum with a battery whose capacity is 25 tons per day. I have not received Mr. Hughes' official report, but the results claimed are fully as favorable as those obtained at Fort Scott. His report will be looked for with interest.

Messrs. Densmore Brothers, of Red Wing, Minn., had an evaporating apparatus at Fort Scott during a part of the present season, and made small amounts of sugar from the diffusion juice of the factory. They have furnished the following report, which will be of interest to those studying this part of the subject:

The John F. Porter steam evaporator deserves special notice in this report. It can be safely and economically employed by every manufacturer of sorghum sirup and sugar. The line of operation employed in this evaporator is that of a shallow body of juice having a continuous flow forward among and over the pipes of steam-heated coils while being purified and concentrated.

The evaporator is composed of two pans or compartments, each of which is provided with a coil of copper pipe. By reason of a peculiar but simple method of applying steam to these coils, the development and throwing out of scum and impurities is begun as soon as the juice enters the evaporator, and is kept up until the juice is thoroughly purged of all impurity. The scum collects along one side of each pan, and within an average distance of 8 inches from the point where it was developed, and is removed from the pan as required by a simple and effective arrangement of skimmers.

While purification has been in progress the juice has been concentrated to a heavy semi-sirup, which is then finished to the desired density.

The line of operation is continuous and uninterrupted, the juice being admitted to and the finished product escaping from the evaporator in a continuous stream.

During the month of September last one of the largest of these evaporators was set up and operated at the Parkinson Sugar Works, Fort Scott, Kans., by the manufacturers for the purpose of investigating the adaptation of the principle therein employed to the manufacture of sugar, and with special inquiry as to the per cent. or amount of inversion of sugar which it might cause.

Four runs or tests were made with this question in view, and the results—given in ratio of glucose to sucrose—were as follows:

Test No. 1.—Juice.....................1 of glucose to 3.24 of sucrose.
    Finished product............1 " 3.05 "
Test No. 2.—Juice......................1 " 3.29 "
    Finished product............1 " 3.27 "
Test No. 3.—Juice......................1 " 3.35 "
    Finished product............1 " 3.36 "
Test No. 4.—Juice......................1 " 3.60 "
    Finished product............1 " 3.53 "

Deductions from these results show as follows: In the first test, a loss by inversion of a little over 1 per cent.; in the second and third tests there was practically no loss, and in the fourth test a loss of less than a third of 1 per cent. The average loss on the four tests was less than three-eighths of 1 per cent. Practically, this process causes no inversion of the sucrose of the juices.

To the wants of the sirup manufacturer, the Porter evaporator is fully adapted in every essential and particular necessary to success. It works rapidly and produces a sirup of bright color and best quality. It is easily operated, and the line of operation is wholly within the control of the operator, whether working for sirup or sugar.

Mr. A. A. Denton made some experiments in air evaporation at the Sterling Sirup Works, and has furnished the following report of his apparatus and operations:

The Sterling Sirup Works have made careful tests of two forms of air-evaporating apparatus in manufacturing sirup this season, and believe the results are of importance to the cane industry, as they show that a cheap and easily-managed apparatus for evaporating at a low temperature, suited to the use of thousands of small factories, may be found in machines for drying or evaporating semi-sirup by hot air; and the method seems peculiarly adapted to the dry air of the Western States and Territories.

The first form of apparatus we used consisted of a liquid-carrier, which had 322 square feet of surface, inclosed in a box or case 3 feet wide by 2 feet, and 14 feet high, placed upon a square tank which held 300 gallons of sirup. The liquid-carrier passed continuously through the sirup in the tank, and its 322 square feet of surface were kept uniformly wet with sirup in thin films by the adhesion of sirup to the surfaces. A fan forced a blast of air through all the surfaces of the liquid-carrier. Hot sirup from the finishing pan was run into the tank, and was immediately spread over the 322 square feet of surface on the liquid-carrier by the motion of the liquid-carrier, where it came in contact with the current of air. The result was that considerable water escaped from the hot sirup in the form of steam, instead of condensing in the sirup, as it does when hot sirup is cooled in the ordinary way, and this increased the density of the sirup. The blast of air also absorbed and carried off considerable water from the sirup, and the density of the sirup was thus increased three or four degrees by the Baumé saccharometer. This was equivalent to boiling the sirup to greater density without the injury caused by the excessive heat necessary in boiling heavy sirup. The sooner sirup is removed from the heat of the finishing pan the better it is, and the sooner hot sirup is cooled the better it is, for finished sirup is hot enough to be injured by the heat it contains after it has left the finishing pan. The output of the Sterling Sirup Works is 2 to 3 barrels per hour, and in previous years we have had trouble and loss in cooling that quantity of sirup in steady day and night runs. The above-described apparatus cools hot sirup in large quantities, and also increases its density quickly and perfectly. It reduced the temperature of 100 gallons of boiling sirup from 236 degrees to 110 degrees in five minutes.

In boiling sirup we usually boil until the sirup has a density while hot of 35 to 36 degrees, as tested by the Baumé saccharometer, but after testing this apparatus we boiled only to 30 degrees, and then reduced it to the proper density by leaving it in this apparatus exposed to the blast of air until it becomes as dense as if it had been boiled to 36 degrees and had then been cooled in the ordinary way. We regard it as an established fact, that sirup at 30 Baumé can be evaporated on large surfaces by air to any density required, and also that the color and flavor of the sirup are better than when exposed longer to the high heat of the finishing pan. By allowing the sirup to remain for some time in this apparatus the sirup was evaporated or dried by the current of air to such density that it was impossible to draw the sirup from the tank through a 2-inch outlet until it had been diluted. All the sirup made this season from 700 acres of cane was cooled ready to barrel and was finished from densities varying from 30 Baumé to 36 Baumé by air evaporation in this apparatus. We next built an apparatus on the same plan as the above-described apparatus, except that it had no fan to cause a current of air; the current of air was caused by heating the air in a furnace, as is done in hot-air fruit evaporators. Hot air evaporates water much more rapidly than cold air, and in operating on thin or dilute sweet liquids it is necessary to heat the air above the fermenting point—above the point where air has chemical action on the liquid. This is shown by drying fruit in air at summer temperature; the product is the inferior sun-dried fruit, because the air has acted chemically on the saccharine liquid in the fruit; but when fruit is dried by hot air, as in the modern fruit-evaporators, the product is perfect, because hot air has no chemical action on the sweet liquid in the fruit. This hot-air apparatus had 273 square feet of surface covered with semi-sirup in thin films, and exposed to a current of hot air which absorbed and carried off the water of the sirup. In this apparatus cane juice which had been boiled until the scum was white and free from green color was evaporated to heavy sirup by hot air. The cane juice was boiled to a density of from 20 to 25 degrees Baumé, according to the quality of the juice, and as was necessary to clarify the juice, and only boiled as long as it was necessary to skim the boiling juice. It was then dried, or evaporated by hot air, at a temperature of 130 to 140 degrees, until it became dense sirup. It is probable that it would have been better to have had a temperature of 140 to 180 degrees, which is the best temperature for evaporating fruit by hot air, and which is the usual temperature in vacuum-pan boiling. In the cold-air apparatus it was necessary to boil the juice until it had such density that air at summer temperature would not act chemically upon the sirup or ferment it, and then finish the evaporation by air at ordinary temperature.

In the hot-air apparatus it was necessary to boil the juice only long enough to clarify it, and then finish the evaporation by air heated above the point of chemical action or fermentation. To illustrate this point: Ordinary sirup may be exposed to air at summer temperature without change or fermentation, while a dilute sweet liquid exposed to air at summer temperature would be chemically changed; but a dilute sweet liquid exposed to air heated to 150 degrees, which is the scalding-point, would not ferment—it would evaporate to sirup.

This hot-air apparatus had 273 square feet of surface, inclosed in a box 3 by 2 feet and 6 feet high. At a temperature of 140 degrees it evaporated 1 pound of water per hour from each square foot of surface—that is, it evaporated 273 pounds of water per hour at 140 degrees. A gallon of cane juice weighs 8.8 pounds. Reducing 7 gallons of cane juice, or 61.6 pounds of juice, to 1 gallon of heavy sirup at sugar density weighing 13 pounds to the gallon, requires the evaporation of 48.6 pounds of water for each gallon of sirup. Where the evaporation from cane juice to heavy sirup is entirely performed by hot air, the hot-air apparatus gives 5½ gallons of sirup, weighing 13 pounds to the gallon, per hour, as the product of the evaporation from 273 square feet of surface in a current of air at 140 degrees. When cane juice is boiled to a density of 20 to 25 degrees Baumé in order to clarify it, and the hot-air apparatus is only required to finish the evaporation, it produces from 10 to 15 gallons of heavy sirup per hour, for the greater part of the evaporation has been performed by boiling.

The hot-air apparatus above described is of a size and capacity suited to a two-horse cane-mill. It would finish the semi-sirup produced by such a mill to heavy sirup, using a temperature of 140 degrees instead of 240 degrees, which is required in finishing heavy sirup by boiling.

The principle of the air-evaporating apparatus is, that evaporation is as rapid from large surfaces exposed to air at comparatively low temperature as from small surfaces intensely heated, and that in evaporating dilute sweet liquids it is necessary to heat the air above the point of chemical action upon the liquid. Solid substances have large quantities of water removed from them by exposing large surfaces to the evaporating action of the air. A bushel of apples weighing 50 pounds is reduced by hot air to 6 pounds of perfect product. The same can be done with liquids under similar conditions. As a result of these experiments we intend to build hot-air apparatus large enough to reduce all our semi-sirup to sirup by hot air next season.

If the question be asked, "Can the farmer *profitably* make his own sugar?" i. e., make sugar for his own use in a small way, I apprehend that the answer should be much the same as would be given to the question, "Can the farmer profitably make his own woolen goods or his own flour?" If, indeed, I have succeeded in the preceding pages in conveying an adequate idea of what sugar-making is, I apprehend that my readers will omit to ask the questions about manufacturing in a very small way.

The farmer who is so fortunate as to be near a sugar factory can do much better than to erect and try to operate sugar machinery on a

60

small scale. An acre of good sorghum delivered at the factory will pay for a barrel of nice nearly-white sugar. The farmer who is not so for tunately situated will probably try to induce some company to erect a factory near him, or will join with his neighbors in forming a company for the purpose of building a factory as soon as the skilled labor neces- sary for its operation can be secured, thereby providing not only his own sugar from his own soil, but at the same time a sure and steady market for the most certain and profitable crop he can raise.

SUGAR REFINERIES.

The sugar produced by the processes herein described is light, but not white, in color. Its sweetening power is not surpassed by any raw sugar, and its taste is very agreeable. The demand of the age is, how- ever, for the best possible goods, and sorghum sugar must be refined to the purest whiteness, and made into the various conditions demanded by the market.

To do this requires the work of the sugar refinery. The largest of the central factories soon to be erected will doubtless be provided with refining facilities, and when located at convenient shipping centers will be developed into large refineries as rapidly as the raw sugar can be obtained to give them work.

CONCLUSION.

There seems to be no doubt but that there is here developed an in- dustry of vast importance to our State and nation. For the year end- ing June 30, 1886, there was consumed in the United States foreign grown and manufactured sugar amounting to 2,689,881,765 pounds.[*] If two thousand new sugar factories were at once erected, and each should produce an annual product of one and a quarter million pounds of sugar, they would not supply the place of the sugars now imported.

The annual consumption of sugar per capita in the United States is about 56 pounds. The population of Kansas may be taken as 1,500,000. These people consume each year $56 \times 1,500,000 = 84,000,000$ pounds of sugar. It will be safe to say that the annual average product of the factories will not exceed 1,500,000 pounds, so that fifty-six factories will be required to supply the sugar consumed by the present population of Kansas, and for which they pay over $5,000,000 annually.

Processes whereby sugar can be made at a profit from sorghum have been worked out. These are far from perfect, but present develop- ments give promise of others in the near future, and will enable us to produce our own sugar on our soil, with the labor of our people. Those who invest in the new industry will be cautious about experimenting with unknown conditions. Kansas is therefore likely to lead in the development, and become the first Northern sugar State.

---

*Address of Dr. H. W. Wiley before the Chemical Society, December 9, 1886.

LETTERS PATENT GRANTED TO M. SWENSON.

UNITED STATES DEPARTMENT OF AGRICULTURE,
COMMISSIONER'S OFFICE,
Washington, D. C., December 10, 1887.

SIR: In response to the resolution of the Senate of the 7th instant, directing me to inform the Senate whether any person in the employ of this Department has applied for or obtained a patent on any process connected with certain experiments in the manufacture of sugar from sorghum, conducted under the auspices of the Government, I have the honor to make the following statement of facts:

For the fiscal year 1886–'87 Congress made an appropriation of $94,000 for "continuing and concluding experiments in the manufacture of sugar by the diffusion and saturation process, from sorghum and sugar-cane." By virtue of this appropriation the Commissioner appointed, under date of July 19, 1886, Mr. Magnus Swenson "an agent of this Department to superintend, under the direction of the chemist, the experiments in the manufacture of sugar from sorghum at Fort Scott, Kans."

In his report to me, under date of December 21, 1886, Professor Wiley, the chief chemist of this Department, in detailing the experiments above alluded to, stated that an acidity existed in the diffusion bath, causing a conversion of a portion of sucrose (sugar) into glucose, and that several experiments had been made to correct this acidity. Among those experiments was one in which he added "freshly precipitated carbonate of lime to the extraction bottle," a method which he states was suggested by Professor Swenson. At the close of these experiments, November 15, 1886, Mr. Swenson's service ceased. On April 27, 1887, he was again appointed "superintendent of sugar experiments at Fort Scott, Kans.," which position he now holds. On October 21, 1887, I was informed that Professor Swenson was seeking a patent for the process which he had suggested as above stated, and while in the line of his duty and which had been tried in a public experiment with the people's money and for the benefit of the country. On that date I filed with the Commissioner of Patents my protest against any action on the part of his office by which Professor Swenson, as an individual, should reap the benefit of this experiment. In answer to that letter I received a communication from the Commissioner of Patents,

61

62

under date of October 26, stating that Professor Swenson had been allowed letters patent on the process, under date of October 11, 1887. In that patent the following claims were allowed to Professor Swenson :

(1) As an improvement in the diffusion process of making sugar, the mode herein described of preventing the invertive action of the organic acids in the cane chips upon the sugar during the process of extraction, said mode consisting in adding to the diffusion bath a carbonate of the alkaline earths, substantially as set forth.

(2) As an improvement in the diffusion process of making sugar, the mode herein described of preventing the invertive action of the organic acids in the cane chips upon the sugar during the process of extraction, said mode consisting in adding to the diffusion bath calcium carbonate, substantially as set forth.

The application for this patent was filed on December 29, 1886, after Professor Swenson's employment by the Government had ceased, but the nature of the claims is so closely allied to the experiment made with carbonate of lime, heretofore alluded to, that it seems to leave no doubt that Professor Swenson intended to cover in his patent the suggestion which he made in the line of his duty, which was adopted during his employment, and which amounted only to an improvement in a process which had been conceived, planned, and was then being perfected by the Government of the United States.

I deem it proper to add that I have had an exhaustive search made of judicial decisions and legal opinions bearing upon the validity of a patent granted under these circumstances, and that I have become convinced that the state of the art, and the fact of Mr. Swenson's appointment and employment by this Department, will affect the validity of his claim, and that I have therefore called the attention of the Attorney-General to all the facts in the case and suggested to him the institution of a suit looking to a perpetual injunction to restrain Professor Swenson from making any use of this patent.

As bearing upon this case, I beg respectfully to inclose, as an appendix to this communication, certain citations and memoranda for the information of the Senate, and in this connection I beg also to recommend such immediate action on the part of the legislative branch of the Government as will enable the Attorney-General, if he has not now sufficient authority, to institute a suit looking to the cancellation of the patent in question.

Very respectfully, your obedient servant,
NORMAN J. COLMAN,
Commissioner of Agriculture.

Hon. JOHN J. INGALLS,
President pro tempore United States Senate.

[Copy of statement of facts submitted to the Attorney-General for his information by the Commissioner of Agriculture.]

Letters Patent, No. 371528, issued to Magnus Swenson.   Manufacture of sugar.

STATEMENT OF FACTS.

The Department of Agriculture directed its attention to the manufacture of sugar from maize and sorghum cane in the year 1877, and since that time has continuously been engaged in investigations and experiments for the purpose of discovering a process that would extract the sugar from these canes in a commercially successful manner.   These experiments have been carried on by direct authorization of Congress.

The first session of the Forty-seventh Congress appropriated, "For experiments in the manufacture of sugar from sorghum, beets, and other sugar-producing plants, twenty-five thousand dollars."   (Stat. L., vol. 22, p. 91.)

The same Congress at its second session appropriated $16,000 (vol. 22, p. 410); the Forty-eighth Congress at its first session appropriated $50,000 (vol. 23, p. 38), and at its second session, $40,000 (vol. 23, p. 354) for the same purpose.   In 1883 the chemist of the Department conceived the idea of adapting the "diffusion process," successfully used in Europe in the manufacture of beet sugar, to the extraction of sugar from sorghum and maize cane.   The results of the experiments carried on in this direction during the year 1883 are continued in special Bulletins Nos. 2 and 3, issued by the Chemical Division of the Department in 1884.

Further investigations were made during the year 1884, and a chemist from the Chemical Division was sent to Europe to study the "diffusion process" as practiced there and the machinery used in its application.   The results of the work for this year are fully set out in Bulletin No. 5.   Bulletin No. 6 contains a record of the work for the year 1885.

In the fall of 1885 Professor Wiley, chemist of the Department, was directed to proceed to Europe to study the "diffusion process."   Bulletin No. 8 gives the result of his visit there and conclusions reached as to the proper adaptation of process and machinery to manufacture sugar in this country from sorghum cane by the "diffusion process."

As a result of the investigations and experiments brought down to 1886, this Department felt convinced that it had reached a satisfactory solution of sugar manufacture, as applied to sorghum, and that it had secured a successful method and devised suitable machinery to establish this work as one of the commercial industries of the country.   To test the process and the machinery devised on a commercial scale, and for the purpose of perfecting by experiments any defect that might arise either in the chemical progress of the process or mechanical arrangement of the machinery, the Department received from Congress an appropriation for these purposes.

On June 30, 1886, there was appropriated as follows: "For purchase, erection, transportation, and operation of machinery, and necessary traveling within the United States, and other expenses in continuing and concluding experiments in the manufacture of sugar, by the 'diffusion and saturation processes,' from sorghum and sugar cane, so much thereof as may be necessary to be immediately available, $94,000."   (Stat. L., vol. 23, p. 101.)

Under this act of Congress the Commissioner of Agriculture on the 19th of July, 1886, employed and appointed one Magnus Swenson to "superintend, under the direction of the chemist, the experiments in the manufacture of sugar from sorghum at Fort Scott, Kans," at a salary of $2,400 per annum, during the continuance of the experiments.   A copy of this appointment is hereto appended.   (Exhibit A.)

The experiments carried on under the foregoing act of Congress last mentioned are set out in detail in Bulletin No. 14, a copy of which is appended.   (Exhibit B.)

In the course of these experiments a difficulty was met with, described on page 28 of Exhibit B, namely, an acidity in the diffusion battery, which caused an inversion of a portion of sucrose into glucose, thereby diminishing the amount of sugar that should be obtained. On the same page are detailed the experiments made to overcome this defect. Experiment No. 4, "the addition of freshly precipitated carbonate of lime to the 'extraction bottle,'" was suggested by Mr. Swenson, the superintendent of the experiments, under the foregoing employment. Comments on the result of this experiment will be found on pages 32 and 33 of Bull. 16.

Experiments at Fort Scott, Kans., were discontinued on November 15, 1886, and the service of Mr. Swenson as agent of this Department ceased on that day.

On December 29, 1886, Mr. Swenson filed an application for letters patent for an improvement in the manufacture of sugar, and on October 11, 1887, letters patent No. 371528 were issued to him.

This patent is for the use of carbonate of lime and carbonates of other alkaline earths in the diffusion bath to prevent the invertive action of organic acids during the process of extraction. It is simply a patent for experiment No. 4, as made at Fort Scott, Kans., by this Department, and set out on page 28 of Bull. 16.

I am informed that Mr. Swenson is now threatening to prosecute all persons who shall use the method described and covered by his patent, and this Department, still being engaged in experimentation for the manufacture of sugar, will be liable to Mr. Swenson in damages for using a process discovered by itself, if the patent aforesaid is rightfully the property of Mr. Swenson.

II.

CONDITION OF THE ART.

The aforesaid patent is for the use of carbonate of the alkaline earths to neutralize organic acids present in saccharine solutions, and thus prevent inversion of sucrose into glucose. This is not new, and has been known to those engaged in the art of manufacture of sugar for years, and allusions are to be met with to its use in works describing this art, and patents have been issued for this same means for neutralizing acidity in saccharine solutions in England. A brief reference to some of these will be made.

In a work entitled "Sugar Growing and Refining," by Wigner and Harland, published in London in 1882, the following allusions are made pertinent to this part of the art.

On page 185, in describing the diffusion process, it says:

"In order to insure the solidification in the tissues of the soluble substance injurious to the sugar, especially of pectine, which is not coagulated by hot water alone, *lime or some other suitable agent* may be added to the water or liquor."

On page 504 of the same work, in speaking of the alum process, it says:

"After the separation of the alum it is possible to *neutralize* the *acid liquor* with *chalk* (carbonate of lime) only, and this has been done on a large scale for a considerable time. The use of chalk has an advantage over lime in that should an *excess* be added it does no harm to the sirup beyond simply *increasing the insoluble deposit in the filters.*"

A description of the identical advantage claimed by Mr. Swenson in his patent, lines 52 to 58, * * * "it is possible to neutralize the acid liquor with some other alkaline body instead of lime; among other substances which have been tried for this purpose are ammonia, carbonate of ammonia, baryta, carbonate of baryta, strontia, carbonate of strontia, magnesia, carbonate of magnesia." These are the carbonates of alkaline earths mentioned in the patent, lines 58 to 63.

In a pamphlet published in Cincinnati in 1876, entitled "Extraction du Jus Sucré des Plantes sacchariféres, par Diffusion," the author of which is G. Bouscaren, is found, on page 2, a description of the alleged improvement patented by Swenson, and it speaks of the addition of chalk (carbonate of lime) to either the water of the diffusion battery or to the pulp of the cane itself before it goes into the battery.

The following is a translation of the paragraph referred to:

"The solidification of the albumen, pectine, and other elements injurious to the sugar being made in the tissue of the pulp itself by the *addition* of a *proper* quantity of *chalk*, either to the water of alimentation or to the pulp itself before its introduction into the macerators."

Of the English patents that have been issued may be noted the following: In 1813 No. 3754, to one Howard, the use of alum, lime, and chalk.

In 1874, No. 1736, to Johnson, the use of alkaline carbonates prior to treatment of the sugar with alcohol.

In 1874, No. 1989, to James Duncan, the neutralization of the free acids arising in saccharine solutions by means of carbonate of lime.

III.

From the foregoing statements the following conclusions may be drawn:

(1) That the above patent is held by Mr. Swenson in trust for the use and benefit of the Government and its citizens, the discovery patented having been made by him while specially employed in experimentation, and under an implied contract granting to the Government all property in the results of such experimentation.

(2) That the thing patented was a suggestion made by an employé specially employed for the purpose, and which only amounted to the curing of a defect in a part of a process already planned in its entirety by another, and which of itself was not a complete invention, and which suggestion would belong to the inventor of the process under whom he was working.

(3) That the patent is invalid in that the thing patented is not *new*.

Under the first head it is sufficient to say that Congress having authorized the making of these sugar experiments at public expense, they are made for the benefit of the public at large, and the results that spring from them become the property of the Government, to the free use of which all citizens are equally entitled. Persons employed in the carrying on of such experiments, so authorized, by the acceptance of the employment waive all personal right to any discoveries they may make in the course of their employment, and by implication contract that such discoveries shall become the property of the Government. It would be incompatible with the object of the act of Congress authorizing the making of experiments, that any personal property to discoveries made by persons employed under the law should be retained by them, for, if so, then the end had in view, the general benefit of the public, would be destroyed, and public moneys would be expended merely to enable private persons to make discoveries for their own personal use and advantage, and not for the general welfare of the people. Congress would be granting public moneys for private use, and this it can not constitutionally do.

While there are no adjudicated cases bearing upon the right of a person employed by the Government to make experiments to discoveries made by him in the course of experiments, there is a dictum by Justice Field, in the case of the United States *v.* Burns, 12 Wallace, page 246, where he says: "If an officer in the military service, *not especially employed to make experiments with a view to suggested* improvements, devises a valuable improvement, he is entitled to the benefit of it, and to letters patent," etc.

This may be held to imply the *converse*, that where such officer was employed to experiment he would *not* be entitled to patent his improvement.

Under the second head, it is sufficient to state that the suggestion made by Mr. Swenson makes a case on all fours with the general doctrine laid down in the leading case of Agawam *v.* Woolen Company (7 Wallace, 583) on the relations between employers and employés, and that such improvement as he suggested would be for the use and benefit of his employer.

The doctrine is thus stated in the opinion by Justice Clifford:

"Persons employed, as much as employers, are entitled to their own independent inventions, but where the employer has conceived the plan of an invention and is en-

15449—No. 17——5

gaged in experiments to perfect it, no suggestions from an *employé*, not amounting to a new method or arrangement, which in itself is a complete invention, is sufficient to deprive the employer of the exclusive property in the perfected improvements. But where the suggestions go to make up a perfect and complete machine, embracing the substance of all that is embodied in the patent subsequently issued to the party to whom the suggestions were made, the patent is invalid, because the real invention or discovery belongs to another," and cases cited.

Under the third head it is unnecessary to comment, for the thing patented not being new, the patent is invalid.

IV.

REMEDY.

The possession by Mr. Swenson of this patent has a serious and damaging effect on the progress of the manufacture of sugar from sorghum cane in this country. It is a cloud on the title of the people of this country to make use of a discovery which the Government has at public expense made. Congress, in authorizing the expending of $225,000 to promote this manufacture, was mindful of its great importance and the benefits to arise from utilizing sorghum cane, which could be grown over an immense area of this country, and make valuable thousands of acres of land, and at the same time cause the production of the home supply of sugar.

This new enterprise has received a damaging blow, and it is desirable that the law department of the Government should take all necessary steps to protect this enterprise, to remove the cloud that to-day prevents the free use of this manufacture as perfected by the Department of Agriculture, and secure to the people the full benefit of all its works.

It is suggested that where a patent has been improperly obtained by a person employed by the Government to carry on experiment for discoveries made in the course of the experiments, the patentee may be *restrained* by injunction from appropriating to his own use any of the rights granted by the patent. This is the view as held by Attorney-General Cushing in an opinion to be found in volume 7, Opinions Attorneys-General, page 656.

PART II.

EXPERIMENTS AT RIO GRANDE, N. J.

REPORT OF H. A. HUGHES.

SIR: I have the honor to present herewith my report, as superintendent of the experiments conducted at Rio Grande the past season, on the manufacture of sugar from sorghum.

The Hughes Sugar House Company is located at Rio Grande, Cape May County, N. J. The building of this company is constructed of brick and iron, 30 feet square, and fully equipped with machinery for extracting and working into merchantable products all of the sugar from 15 tons of cane per day.

The machinery consists of a cleaning and shredding apparatus, a diffusion battery, an open evaporator, vacuum pan, hot room, wagons, and centrifugal.

The cane is cut into sections, freed from leaves, sheaths, and seed tops, and passed in at once to the shredding knives. The leaves and seed tops are also separated and collected into different receptacles. All this machinery is automatic, and the capacity of the cleaning apparatus was proved to be equal to the cleaning of 44 tons in twenty-two hours. It worked without delay or repairs of any description, and the wear and tear was so slight that at the close of the season its condition appeared to be as good as when first started. All this apparatus had been thoroughly tested during the season of 1886.

The shredded cane is packed into perforated baskets and it is then ready for the diffusion battery.

This battery differs radically from those in ordinary use, and was planned in 1886. During this season its work was not perfectly satisfactory—concentration of juice being gained only at a serious loss of sugar in the waste products—but after the close of the season and when the battery was properly managed, it was proven and the tests recorded, which have shown that it can extract practically all of the sugar in the cane at an expense for evaporation of 10 per cent. only in excess of that for mill juice; this result is satisfactory, and is believed to better than that given by any other battery. The diffusion juice from this battery

68

was evaporated in an open pan until one-half of its water was removed; it was then drawn into the vacuum, still further concentrated, grained in the same pan, and struck into sugar wagons in the hot room. The centrifugal machine separated the crude molasses from the raw sugar, leaving it in a condition suitable for refiners' uses. Storage tanks, settling tanks, filter presses, defecators, clarifiers, and chemicals of any kind were not used. The vacuum pan and centrifugal machine do not differ from well-known forms.

THE CROP.

Eighty acres of cane were planted for the use of the mill, and of this 7 acres were grown by neighboring farmers and the balance by the company. Varieties planted were Amber, White African, Kansas Orange, and Late Orange, from which 910 pounds sugar and 80 gallons of molasses per acre were made. In this account is included the unripe cane used in breaking in the house and all damaged cane. The tonnage far exceeded our greatest expectations. This was occasioned by carefully planting the hills closer and giving it good attention, together with favorable rains. The cost of raising the cane was $11.62 per acre. This includes the hauling out of fertilizers and placing them upon the land, which consisted of 150 pounds muriate of potash per acre, and rotten chips from previous seasons, together with a little stable manure in spots. The cost of potash and chips is not included in the above. The cost of cutting the cane and bringing it to the factory was 45 cents per ton. We paid $3 per day for the use of teams and farm hands, and laborers were paid $1.25 per day.

The average yield was 16½ tons per acre. All the farmers' cane was worked and 27.38 acres of that raised by the company. Over 47 acres were left in the fields. One tract (8.43 acres) averaged 25 tons of cane per acre, from which 1,400 pounds of raw sugar and 120 gallons of molasses per acre were extracted.

Part of the field was used in breaking in the house.

The yields of the farmers' crops varied widely, the maximum being 1,970 pounds of raw sugar and 120 gallons of molasses per acre. This was made from 17 tons and 675 pounds of field cane. The term "field cane" means neither stripped nor topped. The minimum was 540 pounds of sugar and 60 gallons of molasses. All the seed used by the farmers was the same. The variations in yield were caused by the difference in cultivation. Other yields were as follows per acre:

	First.	Second.	Third.	Fourth.
Sugar... pounds	1,970	1,560	1,444	1,254
Molasses .... gallons	120	120	60	116

The company grew this cane on shares, giving the farmers one-half the products, viz, sugar, molasses, and seed. The basis of settlement.

was for raw sugar 4 cents per pound and molasses at 25 cents per gallon. Consequently the four best acres yielded—reduced to a cash basis—as follows:

	Quantity.	Amount.	Total.
Ephraim Hildrith:			
Sugar, at 4 cents..................pounds	1,970	$78.80	} $108.80
Molasses, at 25 cents..............gallons	120	30.00	
Joseph Richardson:			
Sugar, at 4 cents..................pounds	1,560	62.40	} 92.40
Molasses, at 25 cents..............gallons	120	30.00	
William Hollingshead:			
Sugar, at 4 cents..................pounds	1,444	57.76	} 77.76
Molasses, at 25 cents..............gallons	80	20.00	
John Brown:			
Sugar, at 4 cents..................pounds	1,254	50.16	} 70.16
Molasses, at 25 cents..............gallons	116	20.00	

This does not include the seed which has not been thrashed.

WORKING SEASON.

The company commenced breaking in its machinery on September 5 and closed on November 8, making fifty-two days. Twelve days in the commencement of the season were consumed in training men to manage the new machinery. The working season was the most unfavorable since 1880. Frost occurred in the last week in September, but did little damage. Ice one-half inch thick was found on October 15. The crop at that time was growing beautifully and the sugar tests rising rapidly, and the day following this freeze the leaves turned white and died.

At that time we were working on the Kansas Orange fields. This variety did not deteriorate for several days, but at the expiration of this time it gradually declined until October 28, when the purity of the juice was reduced so low that it did not warrant our working any longer for sugar. During this period there were several frosts.

Another effect of the ice on this variety of cane was to make it unable to withstand the repeated heavy gales of wind, which finally blew it down and broke it badly.

It was especially our desire to study the effects of frost on the different varieties, and we were fully aware that we could at any time increase our average sugar per acre by leaving this variety and working the Late Orange. After October 28 we commenced cutting on the Late Orange fields, which had withstood frost and ice in marked contrast with the other cane. This variety stood the freezes and thaws with very little change, and at the time of the closing of the house it was still up to the average of the season in purity.

The cane was worked after this date at intervals in the diffusion battery until November 22. The cane brought in at this time was frozen solidly, but the juice was in good condition. Warm weather having intervened from the 22d to the 26th the cane was sampled and tested on November 26 with the intention of making a run for sugar on December 1. Other matters having interfered this was not carried out. There is not the slightest doubt that good sugar crystals could have been obtained until December 1.

This cane has at last been weakened by the unusually severe weather during the past week. It is falling down badly and is only fit for sirup on this date, December 7.

The sugar per acre could have been increased fully 23 per cent. on this season's work by good extraction. It must not be overlooked that the raw sugar made this season would have to be reduced from 20 to 25 per cent. in order to make it chemically pure.

Another source of loss to which I desire to call your attention is in the harvesting of the seed. The seed tops are cut off, spread on the fields to dry, stacked up, and afterwards thrashed. By this method we rarely obtain more than $1\frac{1}{2}$ bushels of seed from a ton of field cane. There is a constant loss in the field during the drying by the seed shelling out and the ravaging of birds. Field mice and rats also attack the stacks. Samples of seed tops carefully saved from these same fields show an average yield, on well developed canes, of 3 bushels per ton. If this seed could be saved it would be of sufficient value to pay the coal bill for working up the crop in this place.

In making the above statements I wish it to be distinctly understood that neither time nor expense was spared in order to make these records accurate; the house being frequently delayed in order that the records might be secured.

I believe that a ton of field cane is too uncertain a factor to be used as a standard for calculation, as it varies considerably in wet and dry weather. Wagons containing 3,000 pounds of cane, as it comes from the field, will increase to 3,400 pounds and more by being rained on. There is a variation in the weight of the cane before and after frost; also in the percentage of leaves of the large and small canes. For these reasons it is better to use clean chips prepared for the battery or an acre of ground.

It might be worth while to state that this sugar house, with slight alteration, could be made to work 25 tons per day, having frequently worked at this rate from six to eight hours.

Believing that sorghum-sugar manufacture is to be an established industry and that reports of this nature will have an attraction for the general public, I have written in this simple style and tried to avoid technicalities. Those who wish the details I refer to the reports of your chemists, Messrs. Broadbent and Edson, who, I believe, have faithfully recorded the workings of the house; also to the report of the experimental station of New Jersey, soon to be issued.

Respectfully,

H. A. HUGHES,
Superintendent.

Hon. NORMAN J. COLMAN,
Commissioner of Agriculture, Washington, D. C.

SUMMARY OF CHEMICAL WORK AT RIO GRANDE.

[Abstract of report of Hubert Edson.]

The manufacturing season at Rio Grande commenced September 5 and closed November 8. The analyses of juices were begun September 8 and continued throughout the season.

On October 15 there fell a heavy frost, one of the earliest known in Rio Grande, which completely killed all the leaves on the cane and stopped the growth of all the unripe fields. The late orange was the only variety which was not seriously injured by the frost and the cold weather following it. This hardy cane, although the frost touched it before it was matured, held its sucrose to the end of the season, even notwishstanding two slight freezes.

It will be noticed from Table III that the extraction of sugar by the battery was very poor. This arose from improper management of the battery by the men employed in the diffusion room, much sugar being thrown out with the exhausted chips from this cause.

EXPERIMENTS IN CRYSTALLIZING SUGARS.

All the sugars as first run from the centrifugal were full of "smear," and after the regular season had closed experiments were made as to the advisability of re-crystallizing the sugar, but it was found that the loss in weight was too great to make it profitable, only 8,329 pounds of re-crystallized sugars being obtained from nearly double that amount of smear sugar.

In Table VIII are found the analyses of the re-crystallized sugars.

On November 19 and 22 experiments were made with the diffusion battery to see if it was possible to obtain a better extraction than the season's work had given.

An extra cell was made and placed outside the battery. Then instead of emptying one cell of diffusion juice at a time the two heaviest juices were drawn into the outside cell. By drawing off two cells at a time two baskets of fresh chips could be immersed each time in the outside cell, and the diffusion juice be brought up within 1° Brix of the mill juice, and at the same time an excellent extraction obtained. Both the days in which these experiments were made were very cold. This, of course, made it difficult to keep the battery at a sufficiently high temperature for a proper diffusion.

In the appended table the degree Brix is all that is given, as the juices were not used :

	Chip juice.	Diffusion juice.	Exhausted chip juice.
Average degree Brix:			
November 19	15.40	14.65	1.30
November 22, a. m	13.42	12.66	1.48
November 22, p. m	15.18	13.79	.88

These experiments were conducted by Mr. Hughes and Dr. Neale, chemist of the New Jersey experimental station. The degrees Brix were taken by Dr. Neale and myself.

A sample of chip juice was polarized and found to contain 8.98 per cent. sucrose, with a purity of 59.27.

RESULTS OF ANALYSES.

TABLE 1.—*Analyses of juice from fresh chips.*

Number of analyses	61
	Per cent.
Mean sucrose	8.98
Mean glucose	3.24
Mean total solids (by spindle)	14.02
Sucrose:	
Maximum	12.28
Minimum	4.71
Glucose:	
Maximum	4.45
Minimum	2.07
Total solids:	
Maximum	17.80
Minimum	10.45

TABLE 2.—*Analyses of diffusion juices.*

Number of analyses	63
	Per cent.
Mean sucrose	6.93
Mean glucose	2.86
Mean total solids (spindle)	11.18
Sucrose:	
Maximum	10.02
Minimum	3.89
Glucose:	
Maximum	3.97
Minimum	1.32
Total solids:	
Maximum	14.40
Minimum	8.38

TABLE 3.—*Sirups.*

Number of analyses	55
	Per cent.
Mean sucrose	18.68
Mean glucose	8.67
Mean total solids (spindle)	32.40
Sucrose:	
Maximum	25.26
Minimum	10.78
Glucose:	
Maximum	15.70
Minimum	3.81
Total solids:	
Maximum	43.16
Minimum	19.88

TABLE 4.—*Exhausted chips.*

Number of analyses	58
	Per cent.
Mean sucrose	2.46
Mean glucose	.98
Mean total solids (spindle)	4.03

TABLE 4.—*Exhausted chips*—Continued.

Sucrose :   Per cent.
    Maximum 4.23
    Minimum .... .81
Glucose :
    Maximum 1.62
    Minimum .... .30
Total solids :
    Maximum 6.64
    Minimum 1.33

TABLE 5.—*Masse cuites.*

Number of analyses 6

                                                    Per cent.
Mean sucrose 55.76
Mean glucose 23.44
Mean water 18.50
Mean ash 4.44

TABLE 6.—*Raw sugars.*

Number of analyses 14

                                                    Per cent.
Mean sucrose 73.80
Mean glucose 13.63
Mean water 5.89
Mean ash 2.56

TABLE 7.—*Molasses.*

Number of analyses 14

                                                    Per cent.
Mean sucrose 35.48
Mean glucose 32.20
Mean water 34.72
Mean ash 5.45

TABLE 8.—*Re-crystallized sugars.*

Number of analyses 9

                                                    Per cent.
Mean sucrose 90.73
Mean glucose 4.63
Mean water 4.19
Mean ash .... .71

(NOTE.—The analyses of *masse cuites* sugars and molasses are only partial. The complete analyses will be given in Bulletin 18.)

ESTIMATES OF COST OF SUGAR FACTORIES MADE BY MR. H. A. HUGHES.

SMALL CENTRAL SUGAR HOUSE.

Cost and summary of machinery.

One vacuum-pan, 4 feet $850.00
One vacuum-pump 500.00
Thirty sugar-wagons, at $14 .... 720.00
Two Weston centrifugals, complete with mixer, at $850 .... 1,700.00
Four tanks, water, sirup, dumps, and extra, at $25 .... 100.00
One 50 horse-power boiler 600.00
One engine, 15 horse-power 400.00
Pipe-fittings 800.00
Two boiler feed-pumps, at $90 .... 180.00
One water-pump 200.00
Two sirup-pumps, at $90 .... 180.00

Cost and summary of machinery—Continued.

Extra work, machinist two months and labor	$520.00
Buildings	3,000.00
Freights, lights and extras	250.00
Total	9,000.00

Capacity of house per day.

Six wagons on 1,080 gallons molasses worked into *maese cuite* for an average, say 4 pounds sugar to a gallon, or	pounds..	4,320
And 45 per cent. sirup	gallons..	488
For 260 days, from September 1 to July 1	pounds..	1,123,200
For 260 days, from September 1 to July 1	gallons..	126,880

Crew, cost of manning, and cost per gallon.

	Per day.
Day shift:	
One fireman	$1.50
One centrifugal	1.50
One sirup and coopering	2.50
One sugar boiler	3.00
Night shift:	
One fireman	1.50
One pan man	1.50
	11.50
Three tons soft coal, at $2.50	7.50
	19.00
Cost per gallon	1.77
Twenty-five gallons for 1 ton field cane ...cents..	44¼

SMALL AUXILIARY PLANTATION HOUSE.

One diffusion battery, 50 to 75 tons, complete	$5,600.00
Cutting and cleaning apparatus	800.00
One double effect	2,500.00
Two juice-pumps, at $90	180.00
Seven small tanks	100.00
One large tank	25.00
Engine, 8 horse-power	200.00
Boilers, 100 horse-power	1,000.00
Two boiler feed-pumps, at $125	250.00
One water-pump	250.00
One hot-water pump	125.00
Pipe-fittings	500.00
Building one-story shed	1,000.00
Labor, freight, and incidentals	800.00
Total	13,330,00

Capacity per day.

Lowest estimate, 50 tons field cane; 25 gallons molasses, 45 to 56 per cent. test for each ton field cane worked; 25 gallons for each ton × 50= 1,250 per day for eighty days =100,000 gallons, or 4 acres of ordinary cane per acre for each day; or 320 acres per season of eighty days.

Three such plants would supply 300,000 gallons in a working season.

Crew, cost of manufacture, and cost per ton.

One man throwing cane on carrier $1.25
One man on seed topper 1.25
One man filling baskets.. 1.25
One man on eleventh cell 1.25
One man hanging on baskets 1.25
One man center 1.25
One man bagasse... 1.25
One man double effect 1.50
One man firing 1.50
One man driving away seed and leaves............................. 1.25

Total 10 men 13.00
One horse on cart... 1.00

14.00 × 2 = $28.00

Labor 28.00
Coal, 5 tons, at $2.50 .... 12.50

40.50

Or 80.1 cents per ton for labor, etc.

RECAPITULATION.

Capital invested, small central house $9,000
Capital invested, three small auxiliaries, $13,300 39,990

Total 48,990

Tons.
Amount of cane worked, 150 tons for eighty days..................... 12,000

Product.

12,000 tons, yielding 25 gallons molasses each ....gallons.. 300,000
300,000 gallons molasses, yielding 4 pounds sugar each..........pounds.. 1,200,000
And 45 per cent. molasses ....gallons.. 135,000

1,200,000 pounds, at 4 cents.. $48,000
135,000 gallons, at 20 cents 27,000
18,000 bushels seed, at 40 cents 7,200

Total... 82,200

Cost of production.

Cents.
Auxiliary house, per ton.................................... 80.01
Central house, per ton...................................... 44.25

121.26
Cost of packages, per ton.................................. 30.00

154.26 × 12,000 = $18,511

Farmers' half, $41,100 or 3.43 per ton; the company's half, $41,100, less $18,511, $22,589 for interest, insurance, superintendence, etc.

In working 1,000 tons a day there should be ten 100 to 175 ton batteries and a large central house. Auxiliary houses of this size would cost complete about $20,000 each and the central house would cost without bone black $90,000. There would also be a corresponding reduction in working expenses.

PART III.

EXPERIMENTS AT LAWRENCE, LA.

The Department of Agriculture having determined to continue the experiments in the manufacture of sugar by diffusion in Louisiana, Mr. E. C. Barthelemy, of New Orleans, was appointed general superintendent of the work January 27, 1887.

Following is a copy of the order assigning him to this duty:

JANUARY 27, 1887.

E. C. Barthelemy, of Louisiana, is hereby appointed general superintendent of the diffusion experiments to be conducted in Louisiana by this Department.

NORMAN J. COLMAN,
Commissioner.

The following instructions were sent with the order to Mr. Barthelemy:

JANUARY 27, 1887.

DEAR SIR: I inclose you herewith your formal appointment as general superintendent of the experiments in diffusion which are to be made in Louisiana next autumn.

At present your instructions will be of a simple nature.

The contract for the building of the machinery has been awarded to the Colwell Iron Works of New York, the lowest responsible home bidders.

This company has also taken the contract of erecting the battery in Louisiana and putting it in order for use.

First of all you will consult with prominent sugar planters and others interested in the matter in respect of the best place for locating this experimental machinery. Keep in view that good double-effect and strike pans and convenient crystallizing rooms, etc., must be had.

I expect to visit Louisiana early in March, and by that time you will have secured such information as will enable me to decide upon the location at once.

Immediately thereafter the machinery and building material now at the "Hermitage" plantation will be transferred to the new quarters, and then the apparatus now at Fort Scott, which is to be used in Louisiana, will be secured. The details of this work I will send you later. As soon as you enter upon the performance of your duties, February 1, you will proceed to Judge Emil Rost's plantation and make a careful study of the machinery on hand, and submit to me, at your earliest possible convenience, a full report thereon, and add thereto your own judgment concerning the suitability of the place for the proposed experiments.

It is my earnest wish that all persons interested in the success of the sugar industry should heartily co-operate in this work.

Very respectfully,

NORMAN J. COLMAN,
Commissioner.

E. C. BARTHELEMY,
New Orleans, La.

77

On February 18, 1887, the following additional instructions were sent to Mr. Barthelemy:

First of all, however, I desire to secure a comparative test of diffusion with milling. When all is in readiness for work, only a few days will be required to make this test, and therefore it would not interfere very much with the regular milling work.

I have contracted for a 12-cell circular battery, to be built on the plan for the Sangerhausen apparatus. All the plans and specifications for the new battery have been purchased by the contractors (the Colwell Iron Works of New York) from the Sangerhausen Company. The battery is to be erected by the Colwell Company, and delivered to the Department there ready for use on or before the first of October. I think it is important to select a place, such as you describe Judge Rost's to be, where all the evaporating and other machinery for working the juices is ready for work.

I propose to make the machinery as simple as possible and to devote all our energies to solving the problem of diffusion.

I expect to go to Louisiana early in March and hope to be able to make some favorable arrangement without delay. The only hope for the success of our experiments is to work with some one who will use every endeavor to make success possible.

The work of the Department will be purely experimental. If it is successful the planter will reap the full benefit of the success; if it is not, no one will suffer any loss.

I do not think I shall ask for more than ten days for the experimental work, and would like to have five days of that time near the first of the season and the other five near the middle of it.

Do you know of any other place where there is a complete apparatus for sugar making which you think would be more favorable than Judge Rost's?

Respectfully,

NORMAN J. COLMAN,
Commissioner.

In March, 1887, the honorable Commissioner of Agriculture visited Louisiana to consult with a committee of the Sugar Planters' Association of that State respecting a suitable plantation on which the work should be done. This committee was composed of the following gentlemen, viz: Hon. D. F. Kenner, John Dymond, Henry McCall, T. S. Wilkinson, L. C. Keever, W. B. Schmidt, J. C. Morris, W. C. Stubbs.

The Commissioner of Agriculture visited, in company with the gentlemen named, the plantations which were thought suitable for the experimental work. After a careful examination the committee made the following report:

Whereas the Government of the United States has determined to test the practical effect of the diffusion process upon the sugar manufacturing interests of the country, and Hon. N. J. Colman, Commissioner of Agriculture, accompanied by Chief Chemist, Dr. H. W. Wiley, having come to Louisiana to arrange for a competitive test with the methods now in use in our State, and Commissioner Colman having requested the aid of the Sugar Planter's Association to select a locality for making the test, the association appointed the undersigned a committee for that purpose. We have therefore inquired into and examined all the places available under the conditions required by the Department of Agriculture.

One of the principal considerations that has guided the committee in making the selection has been to choose that locality which has furnished the most favorable results under the old system, in order that the test should be as severe, as thorough, as complete, and as decisive as possible.

We have examined the various places seemingly available on the Mississippi River, and have carefully inquired concerning those on the Tèche or Attakapas country, and after careful examination and thorough consideration have determined to recommend Governor H. C. Warmoth's Magnolia plantation, in the parish of Plaquemines, as the most suitable locality, from the fact that it would afford the severest competitive test of any place in the State, as the yield on this plantation during several years has been greater per ton of cane ground than on any other place brought under our observation.

March 16, 1887.

JOHN DYMOND, *Chairman.*
D. F. KENNER.
HENRY McCALL.
T. S. WILKINSON.
L. C. KEEVER.
W. B. SCHMIDT.
J. C. MORRIS.
W. C. STUBBS.

I certify that the above is a true copy of the report of this committee made to the Sugar Planters' Association, April 14, 1887.

JOHN DYMOND,
Chairman.

The superior advantages afforded by Governor Warmoth's sugarhouse, the surplus boiler service at his command, and the facilities which he offered for an independent working of the diffusion apparatus were the considerations which led the committee to select his place as the one most suitable to the character of the contemplated work.

At the request of the Commissioner there was appointed by Mr. Kenner, president of the Sugar Growers' Association, an advisory committee to assist those in charge of the work, and thus to help to its successful completion. This committee consisted of Hon. John Dymond, of Belair, and Henry McCall, of Donaldsonville. These gentlemen visited the plantation from time to time during the progress of the work, both of their own accord and by the request of the Commissioner. Following are the reports which they made of the progress of the work:

BELAIR, LA., *July* 15, 1887.

DEAR SIR: In accordance with your request in your favor of 18th instant, I have visited Magnolia plantation, Tuesday, 12th, and Wednesday, 13th instant. The work seemed generally to be well advanced. The house was completed, except the floor. The carbonic-acid pump, filter-press pump, and cutter-engine were all in position and needed only connecting up.

The foundations for the diffusers were being built and will soon be completed. The excavation for cutter was made, but not yet walled up. The lime-kiln was finished, and the washers and connections will be completed this week.

If the diffusion battery comes along promptly, it would seem probable that the whole plant should be ready by October 1, as anticipated.

In consultation with the gentlemen in charge of the work, as you suggested, the matter of a water supply for the diffusers came up. They named 1,200 gallons, I believe, as being the contemplated reservoir of water. It would seem to me desirable to have much more than this, as this limited supply might be exhausted any moment, and it would seem a pity to have the success of diffusion dependent on a water supply which might be cut off in an hour or two from some quite trivial cause. I therefore suggested a 10,000 or 12,000 gallon wooden cistern, which could probably be erected for $200, and this would insure the continuance of the experiments during six or eight hours any way, and during that time any accident interfering with the water supply might be overcome.

As one of the most important points to be determined would be the capacity of the battery for twenty-four consecutive hours, it would be unfortunate to have any stoppage for water.

Always glad to act on your suggestions, I am,

Yours, truly,

JOHN DYMOND,
Of Advisory Committee.

Hon. NORMAN J. COLMAN,
Commissioner of Agriculture.

BELAIR, LA., *August* 2, 1887.

DEAR SIR: I have a letter from Mr. McCall, that he will go with me to Magnolia August 12, and that he can not well go sooner. We shall then report at once to you as fully as practicable.

There is considerable apprehension of danger to the diffusion experiments now felt here, owing to the newspaper report of the choking of the cutters used in Demerara, which cutters are the same used, or contemplated using here.

In response to your request for suggestions, would it not be well to promptly find, by telegram or otherwise, what the exact cause of the trouble is, and whether or not it can be remedied.

This seems to be a serious matter.

Yours, truly,

JOHN DYMOND.

Hon. N. J. COLMAN,
Commissioner of Agriculture.

NEW ORLEANS, *August* 15, 1887.

DEAR SIR: Your favor of the 3d instant to Mr. Dymond came duly to hand, and on the 12th instant we went to Magnolia and carefully inspected the work done and now going on in the matter of the proposed experiments in diffusion, and we would respectfully report:

That we found the cane-cutter in position, as also the engine for driving it. The shafting and counter-shafting are not yet in place.

The boot of the chip conveyer is in position, but the conveyer is not yet erected, nor is there yet any device to deliver the chips from the cutter to the boot of the conveyer, and we understand Mr. Bartheleny to say that none has been provided.

The diffusers were all in position upon the foundations and columns, but were not connected by any pipe-work, and no platforms or floors were yet constructed about them.

The cars for the discharge of the chips were there, but the circular track for them was not yet down.

The cold-water-supply cistern is not erected.

The carbonating tanks are in position and connected together and ready for connection with the diffusion battery.

The air-compressing pump and the air-receiver, to dry the exhausted chips, were there, and the former in position.

The lime-kiln is completed except the placing of the top casting in position and the erecting of the house and platforms around it.

The washing arrangement for the carbonic-acid gas and the pump to force the gas into the carbonating tanks are all in position and connected.

The pump to take the juice from the carbonating tanks and force the same through the filter presses is in position, as are also the filter presses, except one, that we were told was to come from Fort Scott. The connections with the presses were not completed.

The sulphuring tanks, and also the sulphur stoves and sulphur air pump, were in position, and the filter presses for the sulphured juice were also in position.

To write of the matter more generally, we should say that while there seems yet much to do in the way of details, yet we think excellent progress has been made, and that unless some unforeseen delay occurs the apparatus will be ready in due time for the experiments.

The cane-cutter is a beautiful machine, but its complete failure in Demerara, where its duplicate was used, and whence we now have the report of Mr. Quintin Hogg, the proprietor, that it took forty-eight hours to slice 108 tons of cane, indicates its complete uselessness for the purpose, as it is now constructed.

This excites considerable anxiety here, as with all of our machinery now in position we are absolutely without any cutter that can cut the canes.

Other cutters may demand different arrangements of gearing and shafting that might result in delay if not at once considered and provided for.

Mr. Barthelemy thinks that the difficulty with the present cutter arises from the fact that the short ends of the canes can not be held in position for the cutters to act on them, and that a system of spring rollers might be added to hold these ends in position until the slicing is completed.

This seems plausible, and it might be well for you to give him authority to experiment in that direction, but it seems to be almost too late to experiment now, and especially so when we know that the failure of the same machine has terminated the experiments in Demerara, making it a disaster. Mr. Hogg reports they return to the cane-mill process there until proper cutters are provided. He does not seem disposed to experiment with the cutters.

It would seem extremely desirable to provide the cutters that succeeded in Java, as you suggest, and further to provide those you now have at Fort Scott, as you suggest, as the whole experiment may be placed in peril from these difficulties in cutting. We shall be pleased to be of any further service we can, and remain,

Yours, respectfully,

JOHN DYMOND,
HENRY McCALL,
Advisory Committee.

Dr. H. W. WILEY,
Chemist, Department of Agriculture, Washington, D. C.

CANE-SLICER.

In order to secure a multiple feed for a single cutter it was determined to adopt the horizontal disk system. Cutters of this kind not being made in this country, it was necessary to purchase one in Europe.

The cutter built by the Sangerhauser Company, of Sangerhausen, Germany, was selected. This cutter was guarantied to give from 200 to 250 tons of chips per twenty-four hours, suitable for diffusion.

This slicing-machine, having been tried in Demerara in the early summer, proved inefficient. To guard against failure from lack of a proper cutter, another machine which had already proved successful in Java was ordered from the Sudenburg Company of Madgeburg.

The small cutter, with a horizontal disk, tried at Fort Scott last year, was also sent to New York for certain alterations, and thence to Magnolia. Unfortunately the new knives sent with the machine had not been properly tempered, and this prevented the use of this cutter for the preliminary experiments.

Mr. R. Sieg, of New Orleans, who had had large experience in working cane-cutters in Louisiana in 1874 and the following years, was also instructed to build a cutter with vertical disk and multiple feed. We found, however, that the time at his disposal was too short to permit the building of such a machine as he desired.

On October 6, I received the following instructions:

You are hereby instructed to go to Fort Scott, Kans., and after inspecting the work of the Department there in the manufacture of sugar, you will proceed to Lawrence, La., to conduct the work of the Department at that place in the application of diffusion to the extraction of sugar from sugar-cane.

You are also authorized to travel between Magnolia Station and New Orleans as often as may be necessary to secure the proper conduct of public business.

Very respectfully,

NORMAN J. COLMAN,
Commissioner.

In obedience to the above instructions I reached Magnolia on the evening of October 17, 1887. The experimental work was conducted without being complicated by the use of any process or machinery in which any one in the employment of the Department had any patented or financial interest whatever. The sole object in view was to benefit those engaged in the manufacture of sugar in all parts of the country. Experiments conducted at public expense should, in my opinion, be for the public good, and not for the benefit of a private individual or corporation.

On the morning of the 19th the diffusion building was badly injured by a cyclone. The water tank to supply the battery, together with the tower supporting it, was blown on to Governor Warmoth's sugar-house, causing great damage. Nearly a month was required to repair the damage and restore the building and apparatus to the condition in which it was before the storm.

The delays incident to the working of new machinery were numerous. The original plan contemplated having all the machinery ready by the 1st of October, thus permitting a series of preliminary trials extending over a month before the regular season began.

Instead of this, however, unavoidable delays, incident to the imperfections of the machinery and the damage of the storm, postponed even the preliminary experiments until the beginning of December.

A recital of the details of these delays would only lengthen the report without adding anything to its value. It must be said, however, in this connection that the gentlemen associated with me worked earnestly and faithfully through all the discouragements attending the preparation of the machinery.

Mr. Ernest Schulze, representing the Sangerhauser Company, was also present, and rendered valuable assistance in putting his cane-slicer in working order.

The numerous defects in the battery and the cutter having been remedied, the apparatus of the Colwell Company was accepted on December 1i, 1887.

Mr. A. W. Colwell, the president of the company, was present during the final trials of the battery, and rendered valuable assistance in putting it into working order. The defects in both cutter and battery were of a minor character, but were such as to greatly delay the use of new machinery for new purposes. The final working of all the machinery was excellent and satisfactory. The season's experiments, however, disclosed many improvements of a seemingly trivial nature, but by the adoption of which a more economical working of the diffusion process can be secured. These improvements will be discussed in another place.

The first results from the experiments were obtained from the run of December 3, 1887.

The juice was treated with .3 per cent. its weight of lime, and after the precipitation of the lime with carbonic dioxide, an amount of lignite equal to 10 per cent. of the weight of the sugar present was added.

The juice filtered readily through the presses, forming firm, hard cakes. The filtered juice was treated with phosphate of soda, 15 pounds of this salt being added for each 5,000 pounds of juice.

The phosphate produced an abundant flocculent precipitate, which filtered easily through the twin filter presses, giving a juice of remarkable limpidity. The *masse-cuite*, however, was dark, and the molasses much inferior in color to that made by the use of bone-black and ordinary clarification.

The phosphate of soda did not produce as favorable results as had been expected, and its further use was discontinued.

Following are the data obtained in the first run:

First diffusion run, December 3, 1887.

	Total solids.	Sucrose.	Glucose.
Juice from chips:		*Per cent.*	*Per cent.*
First	15.20	12.01	.96
Second	14.45	11.92	1.00
Third	15.45	12.84	1.02
Average	15.03	12.26	.99
Diffusion juice:			
First	10.88	8.88	.83
Second	10.40	8.65	.74
Average	10.61	8.76	.78
Exhausted chips:			
First sample		.51	
Second sample		.76	
Third sample		.91	
Average		.73	
Carbonatated juice	11.09	0.20	.70
Waste water			.12
Semi-sirup	51.80	42.20	3.39
First sugar		97.50	
Molasses from first sugar	76.30	45.00	11.11
Second sugar		91.60	

Cane used..tons..	80.3
First sugar per ton:...pounds..	146.1
Second sugar per ton...do....	40.1
Total first and second sugars..	186.2
Third sugar..	15.0

	Pounds.
The total sugar in the cane at 00 per cent. juice was.................................	220.6
Of this there was obtained 146.1 pounds at 97.50...................................	144.4
And 40.1 pounds at 91.0...	36.7
Total pure sucrose obtained..	181.1
Left in chips...	14.6
Total left in molasses and lost in manufacturing....................................	24.9

(NOTE.—The third sugar will not be dried until in May or June, 1888. The estimates of third sugar have been made by Mr. E. C. Barthelemy.)

EXTRACTION.

The percentage of sucrose left in the spent chips was .73. Sucrose in cane was 11.03 per cent. The per cent. of extraction is therefore $11.03 - .73 = 10.30 \div 11.03 \times 100 = 93.4$.

SECOND TRIAL.

Another trial was made of the diffusion machinery beginning December 9. Carbonatation was again used, but without lignite or any further treatment. The juice passed directly from the filter presses to the double effect pan.

The quantity of lime employed was .6 per cent. the weight of the juice. The filtration was perfect. The experiment was remarkable in showing that a perfect defecation can be made with carbonatation with a much smaller percentage of lime than had been supposed necessary.

The *masse cuite* was dark, but the sugar a fair yellow.

Following are the data of the run:

Second diffusion run, December 9, 1887.

	Total solids.	Sucrose.	Glucose.
		Per cent.	Per cent.
Fresh chips:			
First sample..	14.06	11.70	1.04
Second sample..	15.65	13.64	.76
Third sample...	15.70	13.52	.75
Fourth sample..	15.53	13.02	.81
Fifth sample...	14.00	11.18	1.02
Average...	14.98	12.61	.88
Diffusion juice:			
First sample...	9.36	7.83	.67
Second sample..	8.67	7.25	.58
Third sample...	9.68	7.61	.55
Fourth sample..	10.40	8.69	.91
Fifth sample...	10.20	8.45	.78
Average...	9.66	7.96	.69
Carbonatated juice:			
First sample...	9.12	7.73	.65
Second sample..	8.74	7.35	.57
Third sample...	10.20	8.55	.50
Fourth sample..	11.40	9.00	.73
Average...	9.86	8.16	.61

Second diffusion run, December 9, 1887—Continued.

	Total solids.	Sucrose.	Glucose.
		Per cent.	*Per cent.*
Exhausted chips:			
First sample	....	1.58	....
Second sample	....	1.60	....
Third sample	....	.48	....
Fourth sample	....	.32	....
Fifth sample	....	.40	....
Average	....	.80	....
Semi-sirup	47.70	38.90	2.90
First sugar	....	90.60	....
Molasses from firsts	72.20	42.40	10.50
Second sugar	....	87.30	....

	Pounds
Yield of first sugar per ton	128
Yield of second sugar per ton	43
Cane used, tons	90
The total sugar in the cane at 90 per cent. juice was .... per ton	226.98
Of these there was obtained 128 pounds at 96.6	123.6
And 43 pounds at 87.3	37.5
Total pure sucrose obtained .... per ton	161.1
Pure sucrose left in chips .... do	17.8
Pure sucrose left in molasses and lost in manufacture .... do	41.1
Third sugar estimated .... do	17.0
Percentage sugar in cane extracted	92.16

The poor yield was due to use of thick chips during the first part of
the run, causing a loss of 1.6 per cent. sucrose in the chips.

Following are the analytical data of the run :

THIRD TRIAL.

In this run the use of carbonatation and lignite was discontinued.
The diffusion juices were treated with sulphur fumes until well satu
rated. They were then treated with lime and clarified in the usual
way.

The clarification took place readily. The quantity of scums was very
small, and the sediment subsided rapidly, forming a thin layer on the
bottom of the tank, permitting the clear liquor to be easily and completely drawn off. The juice passed at once from the clarifiers to the
double effect pan and subsequently received no further purification.

Following are the analytical data obtained:

Third diffusion run December 10 and 11, 1888.

	Total solids.	Sucrose.	Glucose.
		Per cent.	*Per cent.*
Fresh chips:			
First sample	14. 39	11. 80	. 79
Second sample	12. 77	10. 63	. 77
Third sample	14. 49	12. 06	. 80
Average	13. 88	11. 53	. 78
Diffusion juice:			
First sample	9. 42	7. 82	. 62
Second sample	9. 41	7. 87	. 59
Third sample	9. 55	7. 86	. 67
Average	9. 46	7. 85	. 63
Sulphured juice:			
First sample	9. 09	8. 17	. 66
Second sample	9. 12	7. 53	. 58
Average	9. 40	7. 85	. 62
Clarified juice:			
First sample	9. 95	8. 21	. 67
Second sample	9. 89	8. 06	. 63
Third sample	10. 32	8. 39	. 71
Average	10. 05	8. 22	. 67
Exhausted chips:			
First sample		. 80	
Second sample		. 50	
Third sample		. 77	
Fourth sample		. 93	
Average		. 75	
Semi-sirup	44. 70	34. 60	2. 87
First sugar		96. 30	
Molasses from first sugar	72. 90	36. 70	12. 07

First sugar, per ton ....pounds.. 143
Number tons cane used.. 110

The molasses from the first sugar was boiled to string proof, and put in wagons. A good crystallization of second sugar was secured but, the molasses having been left too acid, a good separation was not secured. Mr. Barthelemy therefore decided to reboil the molasses with some of the product of the mill process, and therefore no statement of the quantity of second sugar can be given. It was estimated at 30 pounds per ton.

The cane from which this run was made was grown on new back land and was the poorest of the whole season.

The percentage of sugar extracted of total sugar in cane was 92.80.

FOURTH TRIAL.

In this run the diffusion juice was treated with lime until almost neutral. It was then boiled, skimmed, and allowed to settle. The scums and sediments were of small volume and were all returned to the battery.

The juice received no other treatment whatever for clarification. It was converted to sirup in a double effect vacuum pan. The capacity of this pan was not quite great enough to evaporate the juice as fast as furnished by the battery. For this reason the run which might have been finished in two days occupied a part of a third day. The quantity of cane worked was 200 tons.

Following is a record of the analytical data obtained:

Fourth diffusion run December 29, 30, and 31, 1887.

	Total solids.	Sucrose.	Glucose.
Juices from fresh chips:		*Per cent.*	*Per cent.*
A. M., first day	16.46	14.23	.49
P. M., first day	17.27	15.32	.43
Midnight, first day	17.26	15.12	.43
A. M., second day	17.13	14.84	.45
Midnight, second day	16.97	14.93	.54
A. M., third day	16.19	13.90	.61
P. M., third day	16.26	14.05	.50
Average fresh chip juice for run	16.70	14.60	.49
Diffusion juices:			
First sample, first day	9.72	8.71	.32
Second sample, first day	10.00	9.01	.29
Third sample, first day	11.88	10.16	.30
Fourth sample, first day	11.60	9.31	.53
First sample, second day	11.10	9.87	.32
Second sample, second day	10.92	9.69	.33
Third sample, second day	10.94	9.77	.44
First sample, third day	10.45	9.31	.35
Second sample, third day	10.87	9.69	.38
Average diffusion juice for run	10.78	9.50	.36
Clarified juices:			
Average for first day	10.75	9.34	.32
Average for second day	11.77	10.36	.32
First sample, third day	12.01	10.36	.41
Second sample, third day	11.61	9.78	.38
Third sample, third day	11.25	9.51	.36
Average clarified juice for run	11.48	9.87	.36
Juices from exhausted chips:			
First sample, first day		.52	
Second sample, first day		.61	
Third sample, first day		.83	
First sample, second day		1.12	
Second sample, second day		.72	
Third sample, second day		.95	
First sample, third day		1.09	
Second sample, third day		1.30	
Third sample, third day		1.10	
Average exhausted chip juice for run		.91	
Semi-sirup for first strike	37.37	33.10	.99
Masse-cuite first strike		81.20	
First sugar from first strike		98.40	
First molasses from first strike	76.22	51.80	7.76
Semi-sirup for second strike	40.00	35.10	1.19
Masse cuite		80.60	
First sugar		98.90	
Molasses from second strike	79.00	55.60	
Average extraction		93.8	
Pounds first sugar per ton		165.5	
Per cent. sugar extracted obtained in firsts		66.2	

Second sugar per ton .... pounds.. 45.9
Third sugar per ton (estimated).. do ... *18.0
Cane used .... tons.. 200

FIFTH TRIAL.

The fifth and last run of the diffusion battery was begun on January 14 and finished on the 18th. This trial was made after the milling work had been completed. The diffusion juices were treated precisely

* On February 29 I was informed by letter from Governor Warmoth that the third sugars from the fourth run had been dried and weighed, yielding 3,723 pounds or 18.6 pounds per ton.

the same way as the mill juices had been, and after passing over bone-black were concentrated to sirup in a Yaryan quadruple effect, which had been in use with the mill juices during the manufacturing season.

The working of all the machinery during this final trial was admirable, and the even march of the whole work promoted the efficiency of the machinery and the successful manipulation of the juice.

Analytical data of fifth run.

No.	Brix.	Sucrose.	Glucose.
Fresh chips:		*Per cent.*	*Per cent.*
397	16.87	14.23	.74
400	16.39	13.45	.87
403	16.39	13.79	.89
405	17.09	14.73	.68
408	16.86	12.11	.75
411	17.16	14.73	.04
414	16.93	14.06	.70
417	17.00	14.50	.61
420	16.70	13.93	.73
423	16.79	14.11	.74
426	17.19	14.17	.61
429	16.73	14.19	.55
437	17.11	14.55	.01
440	16.17	13.48	.75
443	16.17	13.43	.76
446	16.00	13.99	.63
449	16.63	14.39	.05
452	16.77	14.28	.63
459	16.23	13.29	.77
465	16.03	13.79	.70
468	16.07	13.35	.85
472	16.84	14.34	.64
475	16.37	13.54	.62
478	16.51	14.17	.70
481	16.94	14.38	.65
490	16.57	14.52	.63
Maximum		14.73	.89
Minimum		12.11	.59
Mean		13.98	.70
Diffusion juices:			
398	11.37	9.28	.60
401	10.07	8.66	.64
404	10.01	8.92	.49
409	10.38	8.53	.41
412	11.01	9.10	.45
415	10.91	8.60	.48
418	10.71	8.76	.40
421	10.65	8.77	.40
424	10.57	8.51	.44
427	10.52	8.90	.40
430	10.65	9.05	.32
438	10.27	8.46	.35
441	10.73	8.94	.45
444	10.88	8.99	.42
447	10.5	7.68	.34

No.	Brix.	Sucrose.	Glucose.
Diffusion juices—continued.		*Per cent.*	*Per cent.*
450	9.88	8.12	.40
453	10.87	9.00	.38
460	9.89		.45
466	10.67	8.41	.61
469	10.47	8.01	.73
473	10.17	8.02	.48
476	10.15	7.80	.48
479	10.31	7.92	.47
485	10.59	8.20	.52
491	9.69	7.53	.61
Maximum		9.23	.72
Minimum		7.53	.34
Mean		8.41	.47
Exhausted chips:			
399		.52	
402		.21	
407		.52	
410		.32	
413		.52	
416		.41	
419		.33	
422		.42	
425		.42	
428		.55	
431		.42	
439		.50	
442		.50	
445		.42	
448		.46	
451		.60	
454		.55	
461		.51	
467		.42	
470		.39	
474		.43	
477		.54	
480		.34	
486		.22	
492		.48	
Maximum		.09	
Minimum		.21	
Mean		.44	

The molasses from the first sugars being very rich, the method of reboiling to grain was employed. To this end the molasses of the first strike, having been reduced to 55 to 60 per cent. of total solids, was boiled on a nucleus of first sugar left in the pan from the second strike. In this way all the molasses was boiled to grain with most gratifying results except that from the last strike of the first sugars.

The attempt to boil this to grain did not succeed in giving a *masse cuite* which could be dried with ease. The molasses running from the machines was so thick that it clogged them up. Seven large sugar wagons were filled with this material and set in the hot room.

The sugars made were equal in every respect to those obtained by milling in similar instances. Without counting the second sugar above named, the grained sugar per ton amounted to 181.5 pounds. The grained sugars in wagons will yield not less than 7,500 pounds or 18 pounds per ton.*

The third sugars are estimated by Mr. Barthelemy at not less than 16 pounds per ton.

The total yield per ton of the fifth run will reach therefore 215.5. The number of tons of cane used was 417.

Summary of results.

Number of run.	Cane.	Mean sucrose in juice.	Mean glucose in juice.	Sugar grained in pan per ton. First sugar.
	Tons.	Per cent.	Per cent.	Pounds.
1	80.3	12 26	.99	146.1
2	90.0	12.61	.88	128.0
3	110.0	11.53	.78	143.0
4	2 0.0	14.60	.49	165.5
5	417.0	13.98	.70	181.5

Second sugar.	Third sugar (estimated).	Total sugars per ton.
Pounds.	Pounds.	Pounds.
40.1	15	201.2
43.0	18	189.0
*30.0	12	185.0
45.9	18	229.4
*18.0	16	†215.5

* Estimated.
† Actual weight, 16.3 pounds per ton, and 213.8 pounds total sugars per ton. The third sugars from this run were mixed with molasses from the mill products, and no separate return of it will be made.

COMPARATIVE YIELDS BY MILLING AND DIFFUSION.

The yield in first or grained sugars affords the best comparison of the two systems of manufacture. Judged by this standard the diffusion process had given a yield of sugar fully 30 pounds per ton greater than was afforded by milling. For further data on this point see the report of Governor Warmoth farther on.

CHARACTERISTICS OF DIFFUSION JUICE.

The juice of diffusion differs from the mill juice chiefly in its content of water. In addition to this, also, must be noted a slight increase in the ratio of glucose to sucrose. This is due doubtless to a slight inversion of the sucrose during the process of diffusion. From a commercial

* The actual yield reported to me February 23, by Governor Warmoth, was 6,805 pounds, or 16.3 pounds per ton.

point of view the loss is insignificant. Further, it may be said that there appeared to be in the diffusion juice treated in the ordinary way a slightly increased amount of gummy matter. This was noticed only in filtering the sirup through bone-black. In the strike-pan and the centrifugal the products of diffusion worked fully as well as those from the mill.

DISPOSITION OF CHIPS.

An attempt was made to pass the chips through the five-roll mill, but it was found impracticable. The first rolls would not take them easily, and the second set of rolls had to be opened somewhat to secure the proper feed. The bagasse issuing from the mill contained still 65 per cent. water and made a poor fuel.

It would probably not be a difficult problem to so adjust the mill as to secure a proper drying of the chips. To return the chips to the soil, however, appears to be the most rational method of disposing of them.

It is true that if spread too thickly on the soil the chips may prove highly injurious, but if distributed in a thin layer, covering almost if not quite the original acreage of the cane furnishing them, they would certainly prove advantageous. The chips would not only furnish or- ganic matter to the soil and thus increase its porosity, but they also contain still a considerable part of nitrogenous matter, which would afford a valuable plant food. Even the richest land should be treated fairly, and the cane-field should receive as nearly as possible as much as it gives. The additional cost of replacing the chips on the field is a matter which should receive attention here, but the benefit will appar- ently be greater than the expense. During the manufacturing season the chips can be deposited in large beds, which subsequently can be transferred to the field. If time for the partial decay of the chips should be desired, the accumulation of one season need not be moved until the following year.

DISPOSITION OF SCUMS AND SEDIMENTS.

The scums and sediments were successfully treated by the process of carbonatation. The expense of a lime-kiln is not necessary for this work. It was satisfactorily done by drawing the carbonic dioxide gas directly from the stack of the boilers. As high as 11 per cent of CO_2 was found in the gases from this source.

The scums, etc., treated with 2 to 3 per cent. of lime, are subjected to the action of the gas until the lime is precipitated. They then can be easily and rapidly filtered.

By means of a cheap and convenient *monte jus* the scums and sedi- ments were also returned to the battery. The method of operating was as follows :

The scums and sediments from the clarifiers were collected in a tank furnished with a steam coil to keep them at the boiling temperature.

This tank was connected with a *monte jus* of 50 liters capacity. This apparatus was connected with the compressed-air service used in operating the battery. It was so arranged that the master of diffusion, or his assistant, could operate it directly from the central column of the battery.

After each cell was filled with chips, 50 liters of the scums were run into the *monte jus* from the storage tank, and, by means of compressed air, poured into the full cell. The process of diffusion was then continued in the usual way. The quantity of liquid drawn from each cell was increased by the amount of scums added. For instance, if 900 liters were the amount regularly drawn, 950 would be taken from a cell to which the scums had been added, as above indicated.

No deterioration of the diffusion juice could be detected in using this method.

This procedure was also used during the progress of the work conducted by the Department at Fort Scott during the season of 1887. I have been told that a patent has been applied for to cover this process, and have therefore placed on record the experiments made at Lawrence for the public benefit.

THE USE OF LIGNITE.

In order to get lignite of the best possible variety and in the best form for use, a few tons of the ground article were purchased from the inventor of the process of filtering with brown coal, Mr. Fritz Kleeman, of Schönigen, Germany.

I have already alluded to the successful use of lignite in conjunction with lime and carbonic acid.

This experiment, however, did not show that any beneficial effects were produced by the introduction of the lignite.

Afterwards experiments were made by Mr. Kleeman himself, using lignite alone. Mr. Kleeman said the arrangement of the clarifying tanks was not suitable to the process. The filter cloths were soon clogged and the attempt at filtration had to be abandoned.

Later in the season I received a letter from Mr. W. J. Thompson, of Calumet Plantation, in which he said that he would make a trial of the process under more favorable conditions than obtained at Magnolia, and requesting me to send him enough of the Kleeman lignite for that purpose. This I gladly did. Mr. Thompson made a run of nineteen clarifiers with lignite, but found so many difficulties attending the work that its further progress was abandoned.* On the other hand, Professor Stubbs, at Kenner, working with a small press, secured results that were highly satisfactory.

The results of the work with lignite show—

(1) That on a large scale the filtration takes place with great difficulty, unless a very great quantity of the lignite be used and the juice be neutral or slightly alkaline.

---
* See Appendix B, p. —.

(2) That with a slight excess of lime, precipitated with carbonic acid, lignite can be successfully used to increase the filtering surface.

(3) The decolorizing power of lignite varies with the nature of the sample. In some cases this property is present in a high degree; in others, entirely absent.

(4) The successful working of the process on a small scale would indicate that it might be worked commercially.

(5) In juices as pure as those of sugar-canes, filtration through lignite, even if easily done, does not seem to be necessary.

I had expected to have Mr. Thompson's complete report on the experiments with lignite before this time, but it has not yet been received.

COMPARATIVE YIELD FROM MILL AND DIFFUSION BATTERY.

The comparative yield from the cane-mill and the diffusion battery is given by Governor Warmoth in a paper read before the Planter's Association at the February meeting, viz:

The first cane worked was from second-year stubble, and it gave us 146 pounds of first sugar to the ton and 40 pounds of seconds.

The molasses was put into the cisterns with the other, and we can not give any estimate of the thirds. Our mill gave us 145 pounds first and second sugars from this cane.

The next test was from some green cane, grown on new land, yielding 28 tons of cane per acre—considerably blown down and sprouted in a small degree. This had much less sugar in it than the first cane. Yet we got 128 pounds of first sugar and 43 pounds second sugar per ton from it.

Our mill gave us 140 pounds of first and second sugar per ton from this cane.

The next run gave us 165.5 pounds firsts, 45.9 of seconds; total, 211.4 pounds, with thirds in the wagons, which we estimate will give us 15 pounds more, a total of 226.4 pounds.

The next run was on 450 tons of cane, beginning on the 13th of January, ending on the 18th. This cane was rich and fine. It had been killed on the 26th of December, was not windrowed, but was in fine condition. From this cane diffusion gave us 181 pounds of first sugar and grained seconds, with enough left in the wagons to bring it up to 223 pounds. From this cane we got 193 pounds of first and second sugar by our mill.*

All of this shows about the same difference between diffusion and our mill-work of about 35 pounds of sugar per ton of cane. I do not mean to be invidious when I say that I think we got a little better extraction by our mill than any of our neighbors. My friend, Mr. Dan Thompson, got more sugar to the ton of cane in 1886 than we did, but this result was obtained not so much by his extraction as by the skillful work in the balance of his house, in which I firmly believe the equal does not exist in Louisiana.

It is safe to say that the average yield per ton of cane in the State is not over 110 pounds. I believe diffusion will bring the average up to within the neighborhood of 200 pounds—a gain of certainly 75 pounds, and perhaps 90 pounds, per ton of cane.

* Mr. Thompson's report was received March 5. See Appendix B.

NOTE.—In respect of the last run, the analytical data show that the cane worked by the mill during its last run, from which 193 pounds per ton were made, was richer in sucrose by nearly 1 per cent. than that worked at the last diffusion run.

My nearest neighbor, Mr. Bradish Johnson, obtained the past season 136 pounds of sugar per ton of cane. We are within 3 miles of each other; our land is much the same; our cultivation is substantially the same. It is fair to assume his cane was as rich as mine, yet we had about 175 pounds of all sugar per ton, a difference of 39 pounds of sugar per ton on our mill-work, and about 71 pounds difference on the diffusion work. Take his estate for illustration:

His 10,000 tons of cane gave him 1,390,000 pounds of sugar. Had he worked his crop by diffusion he would certainly have had 70 pounds more sugar to the ton of cane. This would have increased his yield 700,000 pounds of sugar, which, at 5½ cents per pound, would have given him $38,500 more for his crop than he received.

Take my own crop of 13,300 tons of cane. Had I worked it by diffusion I would have had 35 pounds more sugar per ton. This would have given me 465,000 pounds more sugar than I obtained, an aggregate of 2,865,000 pounds of sugar from about 600 acres, or 4,750 pounds per acre. The cash increase of my crop would have been, at 5½ cents per pound, $25,592.50, a difference to Mr. Johnson of $3.85 per ton of cane, and to me, on my crop, of $1.82½ per ton of cane.

QUANTITY OF JUICE DRAWN FROM EACH CELL.

The cane used for diffusion was weighed and delivered, chiefly on cars, to the cutter. The trash which becomes detached in handling the cane was collected in carts and weighed, and its weight deducted from the total. No account was taken of the trash which entered the cutter.

It was found that the average weight of chips in each cell, when filled in the ordinary manner, was 1,757 pounds. One cell filled with extra care was weighed, and the weight found to be 1,860 pounds. It was thus seen that by careful packing it was easy to get 100 pounds extra weight of chips into each cell.

The quantity of juice drawn from each cell varied from 900 to 1,000 liters, or from 2,059 to 2,288 pounds.

The mean quantity of juice drawn for the first four runs was nearly 2,170 pounds. Assuming that in each 100 pounds of chips there is 90 per cent. of juice, we have in 1,757 pounds of chips 1,581.3 pounds of normal juice.

The quantity of diffusion juice from this was 2,170 pounds. The increase over normal juice is therefore 589 pounds, or 37.2 per cent. In the last run a much greater dilution was secured. In order to get a slow current of the juice through the calorisators the master of diffusion was instructed to begin filling the cell with juice when it was about half full of chips. At the end of the run it was found that the introduction of liquid had caused a floating of the chips, and that the weight of chips in each cell has been greatly diminished. Thus a higher dilution of the diffusion juice was secured than was intended. The very perfect exhaustion of the chips during the last run was partially secured by this means.

The mean weight of chips in each cell during the last run was 1,500 pounds; the weight of normal juice 1,350 pounds, giving an increase of 60 per cent. This dilution is greater than is necessary for diffusion work. With a battery of sixteen cells I think the dilution could be easily reduced to 30 per cent. and the extraction be satisfactory.

COAL CONSUMED.

The quantity of coal consumed depends first on the efficiency of the boilers and evaporators employed, second on the quality of the coal, and third on the dilution of the juice.

In beet-sugar factories the basis of computation is generally based on the dilution arising from drawing 180 pounds of diffusion juice from each 100 pounds of beet cuttings. In respect of evaporation what is found to be true of beet juices will also apply to cane juices of the same density.

From the arrangement of the machinery at Magnolia it was found impossible to measure the quantity of coal consumed by the diffusion work. In the last run, when the milling work was over, the centrifugals were run drying seconds and the vacuum pan boiling thirds during the process of the work.

In addition to this, a part of the steam used was furnished by the bagasse boilers, using wood and coal as a fuel—not an economical method of making steam.

As nearly as could be estimated, the quantity of coal required to make a pound of sugar was 2 pounds. The actual quantity of coal which would be required with the best boilers and evaporators may be found by consulting Dr. Karl Stammer's latest edition of "Text-book of Sugar Making," pages 873 *et seq.*

When 180 pounds juice are taken for each 100 pounds beets the consumption of coal to reduce the juice to a sirup of 60 per cent. total solids is as follows:

	Pounds.
With double-effect pan	13.5
With triple-effect pan	9.10
With quadruple-effect pan	6.76

To reduce the sirup to *masse cuite* requires 4.44 pounds.

We find, therefore, the following quantities of coal necessary for each 100 pounds raw material giving 180 pounds of juice:

	Pounds.
For a double effect	17.94
For a triple effect	13.54
For a quadruple effect	11.20

If now we take the ordinary dilution for sugar-cane, the following numbers are found:

In evaporating 180 pounds of diffusion juice from 100 pounds cuttings to 60 per cent. sirup 156 pounds of water are evaporated. In evaporating 125 pounds of diffusion juice to same density, only 101 pounds of water are driven off. To evaporate 156 pounds of water 13.26, 9.10, and 6.76 pounds of coal are used for double, triple, and quadruple effects, respectively. For the same weight of cane chips, giving 125 pounds of diffusion juice, the quantities of coal consumed would be 8.58, 5.89, and 4.44 pounds, respectively. To reduce this to *masse cuite* would require the same consumption as before, viz, 4.44 pounds. One hundred pounds of cane chips will yield by diffusion an average of 10 pounds of sugar for the whole State of Louisiana. The coal consumed in evaporation, therefore, would be:

	Pounds.
For a double effect	13. 02
For a triple effect	10. 33
For a quadrup.e effect	8. 88

The above computation includes the exhaust steam from the pumps, centrifugal engine, etc. The quantity of steam required to run the battery must be added to the above. It certainly would not amount to more than two pounds per hundred of cane used.

With the best apparatus most economically arranged the total consumption of coal per 100 pounds of cane would be:

	Pounds.
For a double effect	15. 02
For a triple effect	12. 33
For a quadruple effect	10. 88

Reduced to 1,000 pounds of sugar from cane yielding an average of 10 per cent. of all sugars, the figures become:

For 1,000 pounds sugar—	Pounds.
With double effect	1,502
With triple effect	1,233
With quadruple effect	1,088

In all these calculations the coal is assumed to be of fair average quality, and to be a'le to convert 6 pounds of water into steam at usual boiler pressure for each 1 pound of coal. In general, then, it may be said the quantity of coal required to make 1,000 pounds of sugar by diffusion varies from 1,000 to 1,500 pounds, according to the system of evaporation employed.

Diffusion can only be made an economical success when the best machinery and the most economical methods are employed. The great objection which has been urged against it, viz, the increased consumption of fuel required, is entirely removed when the process is carried on under the economical conditions which have been mentioned.

To attempt to introduce diffusion with old and worn-out apparatus, defective boilers and open pans, would simply be disastrous. It can only succeed when the highest mechanical skill, associated with the best scientific control, directs all the operations of the sugar house.

In the one experiment where actual weighings have been completed of the whole product, viz, the fourth run, the quantity of sugar made per ton is:

Pounds.

I do not think, therefore, that it is extravagant to believe that with the best culture and most economical method of manufacture the yield per ton of cane in Louisiana may be brought up to 200 pounds. The introduction of diffusion means almost a complete rehabilitation of the average sugar house. It would be unreasonable to expect that planters will have the money and the desire to undertake such a radical change, or at least to make it rapidly.

But it seems to me that the gradual introduction of diffusion, with its concomitant machinery, will work a great change in the sugar industry of the South, bringing success and prosperity where, for years, a hard struggle for existence has been going on.

The final result, I sincerely hope, will bring into cultivation the extensive areas of rich sugar lands now lying idle and increase the production of the State of Louisiana to 500,000 tons annually.

I can not close this report without expressing my hearty appreciation of the support I have received from the sugar planters. The great majority of them were skeptical in respect of the process, but all were anxious that a thorough trial should be made.

Particularly I desire to thank Governor Warmoth for his constant and enthusiastic support and for generously giving $5,000 and more to continue experiments, when the funds appropriated for them had been exhausted by the expensive delays caused by the cyclone and imperfections in the machinery. Without this timely aid the whole work would have been stopped on the very threshold of success.

The advice and encouragement of Messrs. Dymond and McCall, members of the advisory committee, helped me greatly during the most trying days of the work, when it seemed an almost hopeless task to wrestle further with difficulties of a purely mechanical nature.

The active co-operation of Mr. J. B. Wilkinson, jr., was a source of constant assistance during the whole progress of the work, which is but inadequately recognized by a simple sentence of thanks.

Of my own assistants, Messrs. Barthelemy and Spencer had charge of the erection of the building and of the apparatus, except that put up by the Colwell Company.

Mr. Barthelemy took charge of the sugar making during the various trials and Mr. Spencer had the general supervision of the diffusion process and particularly of the limekiln and carbonatation apparatus. Messrs. Crampton and Fake took charge of the chemical work. Mr. John Dugan was master of diffusion. Mr. R. Sieg, as consulting engineer, rendered much assistance. His long experience and thorough knowledge of the literature of diffusion rendered his services particularly valuable.

Finally, I will say that no one recognizes more fully than myself the many imperfections noticed during the progress of the experiments in the machinery and methods employed. I have endeavored not to conceal these, believing that in pointing them out a service is rendered the public only less valuable than that secured by complete success,

APPENDIX A.

Letter of the Commissioner in transmitting report of M. Swenson to the Senate.

UNITED STATES DEPARTMENT OF AGRICULTURE,
DIVISION OF CHEMISTRY,
Washington, D. C., February 2, 1888.

SIR: In response to a resolution of the Senate of the 30th ultimo, I have the honor to transmit herewith a copy of the report made to this Department by Professor Swenson on the subject of sorghum sugar.

For the further information of the Senate I beg to say that experiments in the manufacture of sugar have been conducted by this Department during the past season at three stations, namely, Rio Grande, N. J.; Fort Scott, Kans.; and Magnolia Plantation, La. The two first-named stations worked with the sorghum cane and the last-named station with sugar-cane. I was led to change my original intention to publish the reports of these stations separately by the belief that the combination of the three reports in one volume would make a more useful, practicable, and valuable document for purposes of comparison and otherwise—a document which would be especially valuable in the South to sugar-planters, who might thereby be led to greatly prolong their sugar-working season by planting both the sorghum and the sugar cane.

The material portions of the reports of the two first-named stations were thereupon made public through the press and their official publication delayed, awaiting the termination, last week, of the experiments at Magnolia. The manuscript for this report is now ready for the printer, and it will be published as an official report of this Department within a few days.

Very respectfully,

NORMAN J. COLMAN,
Commissioner of Agriculture.

Hon. JOHN J. INGALLS,
President pro tempore, United States Senate.

15449—No. 17——7

97

APPENDIX B.

BROWN COAL AND WOOD CHAR IN THE FILTRATION OF CANE JUICES AND SIRUPS.

CALUMET SUGAR-HOUSE, BAYOU TECHE, LA.,
Wednesday, February 29, 1888.

DEAR SIR: Pursuant to the conditions attaching 9 tons of German lignite furnished him by the U. S. Department of Agriculture for experimentation in cane-juice filtration at this factory, I am instructed by Mr. Daniel Thompson, its proprietor, under whose exclusive patronage the experiments have otherwise been conducted, to make you the following report concerning the same :

A miniature apparatus comprising mill, steam-defecators, open steam-evaporators, subsiders, and a laboratory, frame filter-press from Wegelin and Hübner, center-feed, executed in bronze, of one-half square foot filtering area, arranged for complete displacement, offered reasonable facilities at all times to small work. Four Kroog presses of thirty frames, 220 square feet filtering surface each, so mounted with respect to receiving vessels, juice, and lixiviating pumps, safety-valves, and like appurtenances as to have operated upon scums throughout the season without suggesting alteration, besides eliciting the eulogiums of the inventor of the so-called Brown coal process, served during industrial trials. All pipes were of copper or brass, pumps of bronze, and the plates, perforated sheets, frames and other iron parts of the apparatus in contact with juice all thoroughly painted, as insurance against discoloration of products. A well-arranged chemical laboratory, unusually well equipped for investigations connected with sugar, was also provided.

Mr. B. Remmers, an English expert in mechanical filtration and sugar refining, well known to readers of the Sugar Cane Magazine, assumed technical control of the experiments, assisted by Mr. R. A. Williams, chemist from the Louisiana Sugar Experiment Station, Mr. J. P. Baldwin, a local adept in defecation, and two long-time employés of the factory.

A preliminary study was made of cake formation. For this purpose Spanish whiting, variously colored, as with aniline dyes and alizarine, kept mechanically suspended in water by vigorous agitation, was pumped into the chambers, the cakes being finished off at high pressures to insure extreme solidity, which, after removal, were cut into sections, longitudinal and transverse. It was found that, with constant or very gradually increased pressures maintained within the chambers, and a liquid kept under unaltered conditions, the cakes formed by extremely uniform accretions, beginning with a thin and even coating of the entire filtering area, over which the various colors used deposited

99

one upon the other, as fed in succession to the press, in likewise thin and equable layers, until the chambers were quite filled and filtration ceased. With oscillatory pressures and with substances of widely differing specific gravities, such as whiting, brown coal, red lead, wood char, and ultramarine, one following upon the other, the various laminæ proved most irregular in their deposition upon the filter-bed, being comparatively of excessive thickness in parts while running out altogether in others, the plane of contact being besides often obliterated or scarcely defined, because of partial intermingling between the different substances employed. The same effects, also, found their cause in the use of any given substance fed alternately in fine and coarse division, or at first in high followed by low percents of the matrix.

There can be little doubt that for the best results in general filter-press work, this indicates, as afterwards substantiated for sugar liquors by the use of hydróstatic columns on the one hand and intermittency secured through means of a by-pass valve on the other, the first importance of constant pressures, freed especially from the vibratory pulsations of ordinary pumps, and a liquid so agitated while awaiting the process as to carry to the press, at all stages of this, a reasonably uniform percentage of whatever matrix is employed, the laws of hydraulics, as illustrated in silt-bearing streams, here again exhibiting themselves in complete application.

Satisfied that the mechanical arrangement of the large apparatus was appropriate to the intervention of a matrix and that the small answered to all the essential conditions of the large, systematic work with brown coal, under what is known as the Kleemann process, began on November 29. Five long tons of this article had been imported by Mr. Dan'l Thompson, through the Sangerhausen Maschinenfabrick, Germany, which, however, was so superlatively unfit for its destined duty, by reason of uneven and inadequate pulverization, as to have required previous and, of course, laborious hand-sifting.

It was first sought to learn what relation varying quantities of this article bore to speed in the filtration of defecated but unskimmed juices. With this intent different percentages, based upon the estimated weight of the contained sucrose, as the most convenient, although not, assuredly, the most rational standard of reference, were employed with the.results which follow:

Lignite, per cent. on contained sucrose.	Juice filtered per operation; 30-frame, Kroog press. (Approximate gallons).		Average time of one operation. (Approximate hours.)		Average juice per press, per 24 hours. (Approximate gallons.)	Average juice per square foot; filtering area per 24 hours. (Approximate gallons.)
	Maxima.	Minima.	Filtering,	Lixiviating and emptying.		
7.5	2,800	2,900	8	3	6,220	28.3
15	2,000	2,100	6	3	5,466	24.6
22.5	1.500	1,600	4.5	2.5	5,296	24.1
30	1,200	1,300	3	2	6,000	27.2
45	950	1,050	1.5	1.5	8,000	36.3
60	700	800	0.75	1	10,275	46.7

The average juice per press and per square foot of filtering surface, per twenty-four hours, stand calculated on the basis of a 60-day continuous run. Here, taking the average weight of the juice at 8.85 pounds per gallon, and its sucrose at 13½ per cent.—for percents of lignite upon sucrose contained may be substituted percents of the same on the weight of juice or pounds of the former per 100 gallons of the latter, as exhibited in the annexed scheme :

Lignite, per cent. on weight of sucrose in juice	7. 5	15	22. 5	30.	45	00
Lignite per cent. on weight of juice	1	2	3	4	6	8
Lignite in pounds per 100 gallons of juice	8. 85	17. 70	26. 55	35. 40	53. 10	70. 80

The juices treated during the interval of this work remained, so far as could be ascertained, essentially uniform as respected adaptability to filtration, as, indeed, they have done up to present writing; being referred in this regard, occasionally, to an arbitrarily selected standard by careful weighings of defecated juice, brown coal, and products operated upon in observed times on tared paper filters. The analyses of raw juices for those dates which cover this series of determinations, as made in the course of diurnal routine work, are presented below.

While they may serve for general comparison with the like as observed in other portions of our tropical cane belt, no relation has yet been noted to exist between the amounts of sucrose, reducing sugars or other known constituents of the juice, and the difficulties exhibited by this in filtration. In the latter regard it is not possible to say if that which has here been experimented upon fairly represents Louisiana's average. It would seem, indeed, to be otherwise, since, in the treatment of scums, great difficulty is reported to have been experienced in almost, if not every, other local factory possessing filter-presses, while at this no other process of manufacture was throughout so satisfactorily performed.

	9 a. m.				3 p. m.				9 p. m.			
Date.	Solids.	Sucrose.	Glucose.	Exponent.	Solids.	Sucrose.	Glucose.	Exponent.	Solids.	Sucrose.	Glucose.	Exponent.
1837.												
Nov. 30	15. 06	13. 5	1. 45	84. 58	.....							
Dec. 1	15. 03	12. 0	1. 31	79. 84	15. 23	11. 6	1. 25	76. 16	15. 43	12. 0	1. 14	77. 77
2	15. 30	12. 1	1. 27	79. 08	14. 78	11. 0	1. 03	74. 42	14. 43	11. 7	1. 33	81. 08
3	15. 27	12. 3	1. 52	80. 55	14. 07	11. 2	1. 47	79. 00	13. 78	9. 7	1. 50	70. 30
5	14. 03	10. 4	1. 62	73. 81	14. 00	10. 7	1. 50	72. 83	14. 01	11. 5	1. 36	77. 12
6	14. 18	10. 1	1. 50	71. 22	14. 03	11. 0	1. 43	78. 40	14. 23	11. 2	1. 36	78. 70
7	14. 03	10. 8	1. 45	76. 81	14. 58	10. 7	1. 50	73. 38	.....	.....	.....	.....
8	14. 43	11. 5	1. 66	79. 60	14. 77	11. 5	1. 51	77. 60	.....	.....	.....	.....
9	14. 63	11. 7	1. 56	79. 97	14. 60	11. 3	1. 38	76. 02	.....	.....	.....	.....
10	13. 06	11. 3	1. 48	80. 94	14. 60	11. 5	1. 47	78. 28	14. 06	11. 4	.....	76. 20
12	15. 00	11. 7	1. 64	77. 53	15. 61	12. 1	.....	77. 41	14. 60	11. 6	.....	82. 85
14	14. 17	12. 1	1. 61	85. 30	14. 93	12. 1	1. 66	81. 04	14. 20	11. 3	.....	79. 57
15	15. 03	11. 0	1. 47	79. 17	15. 00	11. 8	.....	78. 10	.....	.....	.....	.....
16	14. 63	12. 5	1. 66	85. 44	14. 60	12. 0	1. 43	87. 81	.....	.....	.....	.....
17	14. 97	12. 0	1. 61	80. 16	14. 60	13. 4	1. 45	01. 21	.....	.....	.....	.....
19	15. 10	12. 3	1. 35	81. 13	15. 43	12. 6	1. 34	81. 65	15. 20	13. 6	1. 22	88. 94

Average solids 14. 73
Average sucrose 11. 08
Average reducing sugars (glucose) 1. 44
Average coefficient of purity (exponent) 79. 31

Plant cane, 27.5 tons (*circa*) per acre, blown prostrate September 16.

From these trials the resulting extremes, in round numbers, have alone been given. Variations in temperatures and in pressures, both with juice and displacement water; in density and completeness of defecation with the former; in perfection of cake and lixiviation sought, as in other similar variables, some premeditated, others at times uncontrollable, render, as will be understood by a trained experimentalist like yourself, absolutely definite and thoroughly iron-clad figures quite out of the question. The average amounts of juice put through given filtering areas in fixed times have, however, in fact, most nearly corresponded with those presented as minima.

In general, it may be safely said, the most satisfactory filtrations were uniformly of juices slightly acid only, 180° F. (circa), under pressures which, initially low, were most gradually increased until, at finishing-off, 60 pounds per square inch had been attained. Neither reasonable increase of pressure nor higher temperatures than these availed perceptibly. Boiling after the addition of the lignite produced no good result later in filtration, when intimate admixture of matrix and liquid had been maintained. Of displacement, or the depletion in sugar of the cake, more will be said hereafter.

Utterly at variance as the coal percentages and time volumes indicated are with promises which had preceded the process to this country, they proved as persistent as they are disappointing. From 30 to 45 per cent. on the estimated crystallizable product present were shown over and over again to be the smallest of coal consistent with reasonable amounts of work done in given times, with given filtering areas, whether by the experimental or the working apparatus. Upon this last from one to three consecutive defecators, of exceeding 1,300 gallons each, were repeatedly essayed. Separate treatment of skimmed liquors and their scums did no better in the aggregate. Those substances which peculiarly interfere with filtration appear to be removed only in minimum degree with the skimmings and sediments. Were this otherwise, separation and recovery of juice from the latter by filter-pressing, as now practiced, would scarcely be feasible. It was the same whether with a lime, a sulphurous acid and lime, a lime and phosphoric acid, an acid sulphite of alumina, or an acid albumen defecation, under the Willcox patent; and with these reagents in all proportions. Tannic acid extracted coloring matter from the brown coal, as did phosphoric and some other chemicals, without facilitating filtration. The use of lignite in alkaline solution is forbidden by its solubility in such. Basic lead acetate showed no better effects with the small press than the rest. Carbonatation alone succeeds, and this, as you told me, requires no lignite. Repetition, later repeated, with foreign lignite prepared under Mr. Kleemann's individual supervision and furnished by your department, as also with native coals obtained from the Louisiana Sugar Experiment Station and other sources, comminuted at home, aggravated the disappointment. All degrees of pulverization were tried. The amounts filtered seemed tolerably constant for stubble and plant-cane juices and for juices from freshly cut canes, and from those many weeks windrowed. From old land cane they did doubtfully better than from new; those deteriorated as a frost effect not altogether so well, perhaps, as those not so injured. With cane freed from its adhering cerosin, by sand-papering prior to crushing, it went no better. Butts showed no decided superiority to middles and tops.

In all cases the filtered juices, whether from skimmed liquors or scums or the two treated without previous separation, whether from high or low percentages of brown coal and with whatever defecating agent employed, were exceedingly bright and clear from the first until running had quite ceased altogether. Another disappointment, however, awaited inquiry into the actual improvement as to purity secured. The exponent, on the average, was raised not materially to exceed one per cent. of total solids attributable to the coal, exclusive even of sweet-waters. A few analyses, taken at random from the laboratory records, sufficiently illustrate this. In every case the non-filtered and filtered samples represent, as nearly as practicable, the same juice. For the large presses these were taken in equal volumes at the discharge openings of defecators and presses, respectively, at intervals of three minutes, always so as to represent by pairs identical defecators of juice and identical defecations, before and after filtration, which, following adequate admixture of each series, as obtained from individual defecators, were re-sampled. This was permitted by the admirable arrangement of the coal-mixing receivers, which contained, each, precisely the amount from one defecator, and which were filled and emptied alternately in rotation. The effect of a thorough cake washing, the sweet-water being mixed back proportionately with the filtered juice, of which it was the after-product, is shown in the last two analyses.

Date.	Defecated, not filtered.					Filtered, 30 to 45 per cent. brown coal.					Improvement in exponent.	Remarks.
	Solids.	Sucrose.	Glucose.	Exponent.	Glucose ratio.	Solids.	Sucrose.	Glucose.	Exponent.	Glucose ratio.		
1887.												
Dec. 28	16.44	13.0	1.84	79.08	14.15	16.43	13.3	1.80	80.95	14.15	1.87	Frosted cane.
28	16.44	13.0	1.84	79.08	14.15	16.03	12.9	1.78	80.47	13.79	1.39	Cake from the above used.
29	16.44	13.6	1.46	82.72	10.70	16.44	13.8	1.38	83.94	10.00	1.22	
30	17.05	13.0	1.25	81.52	8.99	16.48	13.6	1.19	82.52	8.75	1.00	Willcox albumen defecation.
31	15.00	11.7	1.44	78.00	12.30	14.70	11.6	1.40	78.91	12.07	0.91	
1888.												
Jan. 2	15.00	12.6	1.20	84.00	9.52	15.30	13.0	1.30	84.97	10.00	0.97	
3	15.17	12.3	1.07	81.08	8.69	15.20	12.6	1.10	82.89	8.00	1.81	
4	15.11	12.3	1.19	81.40	9.07	14.56	12.0	1.13	82.41	9.41	1.01	
10	16.46	13.5	1.00	82.01	7.41	15.96	13.3	1.01	83.33	7.52	1.32	Large presses, Willcox defecation.
17	16.44	13.5	1.10	82.11	8.17	15.12	12.6	1.02	83.33	8.09	1.22	Large presses, lime defecation.
17	16.63	13.6	0.96	81.77	7.06	15.67	12.9	0.83	82.32	6.43	0.55	Large presses.
17	16.47	13.5	1.00	81.96	7.40	15.57	12.8	0.89	82.21	6.05	0.25	Large presses, pro rata of sweet H_2O included.
17	16.36	13.0	1.06	83.12	7.79	15.29	12.9	0.94	84.37	7.28	1.25	Large presses.
17	16.36	13.0	0.91	79.46	7.00	15.34	12.2	0.83	79.53	6.80	0.07	Large presses, pro rata of sweet H_2O included.
17	15.90	13.4	0.98	84.27	7.35	14.76	12.5	0.90	84.57	7.20	0.30	Do.
Means.	16.08	13.1	1.22	81.46	9.31	15.52	12.8	1.16	82.47	9.06	1.01	

After that, due to the use of 10 or 15 per cent of lignite on the weight of sugar present, no commensurate effect was observed to be produced in the direction of increased purity by the addition of further quantities. This fell off very slightly or not at all, however, as filtration proceeded towards its finishing point, as also more or less in lixiviation, depending, as seemed shown, upon a lower or higher percentage of coal employed. Believing the application of the process to Louisiana juice, condemned by the excessive quantities of lignite found essential to sufficiently rapid filtration and by its failure to realize a higher gain in purity, before reaching conclusive knowledge of these minutiæ it should be said these have not since been accorded that systematic inquiry which, otherwise, they would have deserved.

As decolorizers of saccharine liquors, either dilute or concentrated, certain brown coals are, on the other hand, surprisingly effective. In the table annexed are given to the nearest per cent, the color repeatedly removed from defecated juices, by varying percentages of the article furnished by your Department, referred in each series to standard samples prepared from the defecated juice dealt with by mere passage through filter paper. This paper filtration is a necessity, since suspended matter, lighter in color than the mother-liquor, partially by preventing the transmission of light through this last and partly by itself reflecting light, gives invariably, in simply subsided juices, a tint too light by a number of degrees. The percentages of color removed were uniformly measured by the relative length of columns made to give the same tint as the untreated standard when contained in tubes of like glass, of caliber such as to avoid a decided meniscus, and with light of equal intensities transmitted from below in lines parallel to the columns' longitudinal axes.

Lignite, per cent. on weight of sucrose.	Length of columns mm.	Per cent. color removed.
Unfiltered	10	....
5	28	64
10	36	72
15	50	80
20	64	84
25	80	88
30	92	89
40	100	90
50	112	91

In the foregoing the juices were treated nearly to neutrality with lime alone. With sulphurous and phosphoric acids, acid albumen, acid sulphite of alumina, or even a decidedly acid lime defecation, the per cents. removed were, of course, reduced, there being a less intense primary tint. No other lignite gave such high effects as that furnished by your Department. This will be seen from the accompanying approximatious, obtained with from 22.5 per cent. to 25.0 per cent. of lignite on the weight of sucrose filtered, expressed in maxima and minima to the nearest 10, sulphur fumes having been used on the juices—the sir-, ups not having been treated with coal prior to concentration.

Lignite, where obtained.	Per cent. color removed.			
	Juice.		Sirup.	
	Maxima.	Minima.	Maxima.	Minima.
Sangerhausen Machine Works, Germany	60	40	45	35
United States Department of Agriculture, prepared by F. Kleemann, Germany	80	60	50	40
Louisiana Sugar Experiment Station, mined in Alabama	70	50	45	35
J. B. Friedleim, Camden, Ark	60	40	40	30
B. F. Read & Co., Mineola, Tex	60	40	40	30

The higher effect of your article is perhaps attributable, in considerable measure, to a more perfect pulverization than that secured in other samples, the degree of this exercising an undoubted influence. As was noticed in the matter of purity coefficient, after the use of some 15 per cent further amounts added were out of all proportion to the increase in effect. The power of lignite to absorb or otherwise destroy or remove is apparently confined to those contained substances producing particular color effects only. For these its affinity is certainly very great, animal char or bone black, in the lower percentages, being found altogether out of comparison with it in this regard. These colors suppressed, however, by a relatively small quantity of the lignite, additional quantities produce but little useful effect, the remaining coloring matters being those for which it possesses little or no affinity. This hypothesis explains the fact that, having used so much as 30 to 45 per cent. to secure rapidity of filtration, the cake from one operation was found to have lost none of its decolorizing power upon a second application, though it no longer filtered with the same efficiency. Its influence upon the exponent, also, seemed to have diminished little by like previous use upon juice, although considerably more so after the filtration of dense sirups not first treated as juice, a fact possibly finding its explanation on the same lines. Except for the Texas sample, all the coals examined gave up a slight amount of greenish coloring matter, whether boiled in distilled water, juice, or sirup, all showing likewise an acid reaction, your own being most pronounced in the latter particular.

A hard and apparently very dry cake was obtained with whatever variety of lignite, if employed in amounts above 15 per cent. of the contained sugar, provided only ample time was accorded its formation. It was, however, in all instances of high per cents, exceedingly porous as compared with scum cake finished off at corresponding pressures, weighing per press always in close proximity to the ascertained average of 670 pounds at a final pressure of 60 pounds, of which, after lixiviation at 40 pounds pressure, 49 per cent., a little more or less, was moisture.

Since with a juice polarizing 13 per cent. sucrose some 46 pounds of the latter would be otherwise lost from each pressing, equal to nearly 3 per cent. of the entire amount treated, supposing 1,300 gallons of juice to be put through, with 30 per cent. of the brown coal, at each operation, the importance of lixiviation can scarcely be overstated. No press except arranged for this supplementary process in its most complete attainment would, of course, be admissible. This work is too ununiformly accomplished by steam, by reason of channels at once cut on lines of least resistance, which, besides, leaves the press too hot for immediate manipulation and severely taxes the cloths. Hot water results in too rapid and too great a reduction of the purity coefficient, possibly because of the action of heat upon the solubility of some among the retained impurities. Cold water certainly performed best, all things considered.

The theoretical amount of so-called displacement water was found altogether inadequate. For a 30-frame Kroog press 200 liters are, for reasons not necessary to state, supposed to be the extreme limit of requirement. This amount when passed in one hour—already a serious loss of time compared with the filtration itself, which consumes but three with 30 per cent. of coal—gave at finishing-off a sweet-water still running at an average analysis of: solids, 6.77; sucrose, 5.0; reducing sugars, 0.52; exponent, 73.87. Assuming the 49 per cent. of retained moisture on the 670 pounds of cake to be juice diluted to the same figures, we should have:

	Pounds.
As water	328. 30
As contained solids	23. 83
As dilute juice	352. 13

equal to 25.5 per cent. of the cakes' weight, which would mean the loss per operation of $670 \times 0.525 \times 0.05 = 17.58$ pounds sucrose, or $352 \times 0.05 = 17.60$ pounds sucrose, or to $17.60 \times 46.1 = 811.36$ pounds sucrose per day's work of 60,000 gallons of juice, using 30 per cent. of lignite.

As a matter of fact, analysis of the cake showed this to contain 2.8 per cent. sucrose, or 18.76 pounds, of the latter per pressing—a seeming paradox, dispelled by physical examination. This sufficed to reveal how the water, first finding its way past the cake on its line of contact with the iron frame, thoroughly lixiviated the extreme peripheral portions of this, afterwards to pass here in important volumes without effecting any good purpose, while yet having accomplished only a very partial depletion of more central parts. Here was met the third and last serious technical objection to lignite; one which, since it is multiplied by the number of pressings required for given volumes of juice filtered, must apply to the use of any matrix just in proportion as larger or smaller amounts of this are essential to the results sought.

There appeared to offer two methods of escape from this difficulty, each, however, involving a dilemma. Lower lixiviating pressures, while producing much better effects, prolonged the time required for the operation so far beyond the reasonable as would need double or treble the filter-press plant. Increased quantities of water employed reduced the exponent, prolonged the time, and increased the evaporation correspondingly. A third expedient was less effective, but offered some collateral advantages, to wit, more perfect pulverization of the matrix. There can be no reasonable doubt that the finer the state of division to which brown coal is reduced the more rapid becomes filtration, the more complete the decolorization effected, the more solid its cake, and the lower its final per cent. of retained juice. Sifted through the finest of millers' silk bolting-cloth, it performs better duty in every respect than otherwise. It is advisedly stated, and with positiveness, after repeated experiment, that lignite can not be too finely prepared, on a large scale at least, for cane-juice filtration, by any mechanical means at present command. Dissolved even in strong alkalis and reprecipitated as an impalpable powder, its efficiency is yet further enhanced.

As a last recourse higher juice pressures, even up to 300 pounds per square inch on the small press, were used. This, though it unquestionably left remaining a cake charged likewise with less juice and so uniformly compact as to be better adapted to displacement, again was attended with too serious a loss of time, both in finishing off and in subsequent lixiviation, to compensate the advantage in sugar redeemed or evaporation avoided. Pressures in excess of 100 pounds per square inch are, besides, not feasible in industrial practice.

A single industrial run of twenty-four hours was finally made January 16th and 17th with brown coal, with intent primarily to develop and locate any unforeseen mechanical difficulties incident to continuous work. Numerous such arose, of course, each happily, however, suggesting at once its own certain remedy. If, technically, this large effort was not as satisfactory as might have been anticipated from the painstaking arrangements made for and well-organized and precise management accorded it, it was yet successful beyond all expectation in solving those problems which must ever attach in cane-juice work to the application in filter-presses on a considerable manufacturing basis, of any matrix whatever. It removed at a stroke all necessity for the yet more extensive operations which, as you know, had previously been proposed.

It is needless here to weary you with the details of this day's run, which, with its antecedents rather than with its consequents, demonstrated conclusively, as is believed, that while the filtration of the entire body of defecated juice thus, with brown coal, stands well among the mechanical possibilities, its application can by no means now conceived with us be rendered remunerative to the Louisiana industry. This your discernment will already have made quite as clear to you by what precedes, as it can by any present comparison between the weights and polarizations of its resulting products and those customary to the establishment in its treatment of like raw materials. Such data, indeed, await your command, but indicate to me no variation in *rendement* beyond that attributable to the accidents and incidents common with every-day factory experience. There occurred nothing of the oft and persistently predicted clogging, either of pumps, conduits, presses, or cloths. The cloths at the end of twenty-four hours showed no loss of transmitting power, and were washed with surprising ease.

In quality of products, no doubt, some advantage was recognized to accrue, bone-coal not being employed in the factory. Notwithstanding, in this particular also, disappointment was felt. In no other respect than this, surely, did the results of this experiment compare even favorably with those secured by Mr. G. L. Spencer, in 1886, with the Remmers and Williamson wood-char process, under the patronage of your Department at its Magnolia Station, as these stand officially reported in your Bulletin No. 15 (pp. 20–25, inclusive). So much more effective has vegetable char than brown coal been shown also in our own work, both as a filtering and as a defecating agent, that, having abandoned the latter altogether, experimentation since several weeks with the former, in a laboratory way, with seed-cane, has now been in seemingly successful progress here. The following is not an unfair comparison, so far as experience yet teaches, between the two articles applied to juices somewhat deteriorated by long storage of canes:

	Matrix required on weight of sucrose.	Improvement of purity coefficient.	Decolorization sulphured.
	Per cent.		*Per cent.*
Brown coal	30 to 45	0. 30 to 1. 90	60 to 80
Wood char	6 to 12	1. 50 to 4. 30	6 to 12

Liguite presents other disadvantages, as well, in comparison with wood charcoal. Upon concentration to sirup, juice filtered with whatever percentage of it, whether reduced with the low temperatures of vacuum evaporation or under atmospheric pressure, gives invariably an additional precipitate of matter probably rendered insoluble solely by the increase of density. No such precipitate has at any time, with any defecating agent, been observed after filtration with wood coal. How weak is its absorptive power, beyond that for coloring matters, is shown by the fact that, after filtration through paper alone, an improvement of but 0.03 in the exponent was secured to sirups from the ordinary lime

108

defecation by subsequent treatment with 30 per cent. of the lignite.
Below are the averages:

[Concentrated in double effect.]

Sirup.	Solids.	Sucrose.	Glucose.	Exponent.	Glucose ratio.
After primary filtration through paper	57.60	47.2	4.55	81.94	0.64
After subsequent treatment with 30 per cent. lignite	62.70	51.4	4.76	81.97	0.58
Rise in purity coefficient with lignite				0.03	

Although when freshly ground, and yet containing from 30 to 35 per
cent. of hyroscopic moisture, it can be readily brought to mix intimately
by mechanical means with the juices, this is scarcely to be accomplished
in the large and regular quantities required if, having been long prepared, desiccation to 15 or 20 per cent. has not somehow been prevented;
in which state, if sufficiently comminuted, it excels not only the kneading
requirements of patent flour fourfold but becomes even dangerous from
liability to spontaneous combustion. This infers the necessity for a
grinder on the premises, with engine, foundations, sifters, elevators, mix-
ers, shafting, belting, and their like ad libitum, in a structure apart from
the factory building proper, which last would needs be protected from the
attendant dust, as another serious sugar-making complication and care.
Such a plant has been estimated, by a probably competent European
engineer, to cost, for a 60,000-pound diurnal output, erected upon this
property, exclusive of the presses and their immediate appurtenances,
but inclusive of building, not less than $10,000. Wood coal can, on the
other hand, safely be prepared during the leisure of idle months, at
home or elsewhere, and be mixed in the greatly reduced amounts called
for, as wanted, with the most simple and inexpensive devices or be
stored without injury or danger from season to season. Even wood
char, however, for satisfactory filtration, should also contain a considerable percentage of moisture when ground. Otherwise the first
run of liquor is likely to come charged with the char, requiring refiltra-
tion. It appears that this, unlike lignite, may be rendered in part too
pulverulent, which last the enforced presence of sufficient moisture at
the time of its reduction is believed to prevent.
Brown coal, again, is not known to exert even a favorable mechanical action on the soil's productiveness; that wood char exercises valuable functions in this regard is well understood among agronomists.
If in the ordinary filter-pressing of scums and sediments well-nigh the
entire fertilizing content of the juice itself is already secured, leaving no
credit for such properly to be conceded to either, for this mechanical advantage of charcoal something may well be deducted from its estimated
first cost to manufacture. It presumably absorbs from the juice, also,
fertilizing material in excess of the brown coal, equivalent to the additional rise it secures in the exponent of this. The aggregate bulk of
brown coal required would be such as might well preclude economic
distribution over the fields.
Considering the quality of the native brown coals as yet examined,
the cost of transportation, and, if imported, the duty upon such enor-
mous quantities of these as are demanded, the price of vegetable char,
it appears, should compare most favorably with them throughout the

Louisana sugar belt. Brown coal, in sugar work, demands also a royalty under letters patent; the patents upon wood char, in this application, have been permitted to lapse. Brown coal can not be revivified. Wood char, it is believed, can be reburned by superheated steam in any state of comminution, if found desirable. It remains to be known from the distillation of which variety of wood, however, the best quality of the last-named article for the purpose proposed is to be obtained. As saw-dust, oak is known to perform best, probably because of its excess in tannic acid.

As of application with whatever matrix employed it is pertinent only to add, as a further result of our experience in the matter, a few convictions touching the appliances best suited to the treatment of juice in considerable volumes.

The advantage of duplex, double-acting plunger pumps, extra large for their duty and operated at low-piston speeds, with exceedingly capacious air vessels and sensitive safety-valves placed close to the pumps, the last of equal conducting capacity with the feed-pipes, was fully indicated. To thus insure, by every means, against sudden variations of pressure, such, especially, as the vibratory pulsations inseparable from ordinary pumping plants, seemed essential to a cake of maximum uniformity and uniformly well adapted to lixiviation in all its parts, as before insisted. With the lixiviating apparatus itself this completeness in erection is even more prominently to be indorsed, except that, as no grit is here to be encountered, piston-pumps should suffice. A continuous stream of liquid running from the safety-valves, both juice and lixiviating, should be maintained during operation. In the most perfect practice no approach to theoretical displacement has been found to occur. This supplementary process is, unfortunately, at the most we have been able to make it, little more than has been expressed with the word lixiviation. Whiting and highly colored liquids render its study facile.

The absolute necessity to the process of chamber presses, whether top, bottom, or central feed, and, conversely, the total unsuitability of frame-presses in general to it, was left in no doubt. Each operation consumes so short an interval that a large percentage of total time is spent in emptying. A chamber-press can be emptied readily in one-half the period consumed by one of the frame variety for the same number of cakes. As the cloths need be removed not oftener than twice a week the loss from this source, in employing such, is negligible. It is not true that cloths wear most rapidly from use in chamber presses, except these be ill-constructed. The tendency during lixiviation which the water exhibits, however this be fed and no matter how superlatively perfect the cake is, to cut of itself a ready and continuous channel about the cake's peripheral joint with the iron frame, has been mentioned. This results in a sludge formed along the cake's feather edges which, upon opening the press, runs more or less, despite the best effort, down the frame's sides, especially along its bottom portions, compromising the joint which this afterwards makes with its adjoining cloth Following three rounds with brown coal, such a press can not be made tight and after four or five may even refuse to close, except the surfaces be laboriously cleansed with iron scrapers. In chamber presses the peripheral joint is made between cake and cloth and not between cake and iron. From this fact alone it is far more perfect. Its form, however, if properly designed, is of yet greater importance and, presenting no longer necessarily a line of least resistance, reduces the chance of sludge, besides insuring, other things equal, a more uniform and complete displacement with reduced quantities of water by preventing the formation of such water channels as those before described. If, by any chance, a small amount of semi-liquid material here runs in like manner, notwithstanding, this interferes in but half degree with a press joint now made between two thicknesses of the fabric instead of between iron and one such. Although in top and bottom fed chamber presses the liquor inter-ports of the individual chambers may be of greater diameter than those possible with frames, yet from liability to obstruction the center feed is to be preferred.

Any filter-press constructed for the use of brown coal or any of its congeners should be recessed for $1\frac{1}{4}$ instead of for 1 inch cakes. This statement will not remain true except that in all cases the wisdom of employing the matrix in excess in confirmed. A yet greater thickness in these might then perhaps prove still more advantageous were it not the limit at which, in such presses, the cloths have been made to stand. Without attempting an explanation of the fact it remains that with chambers of increased thickness higher results per square foot of filtering area are attained, this dimension even doubled, curiously enough as it would seem, requiring but a very small fraction more of time for cake completion than before, so long as a slight excess only of matrix is in each instance employed. This is best illustrated in starch manufacture. Speed in filtration is, then, increased by this innovation, except for deficiency of matrix; a relative reduction in the amount of sweet-water to be dealt with is secured and proportionate time is saved in emptying.

Since it consumes no more time to empty thirty chambers presenting 400 square feet of filtering area than thirty aggregating but 220, presses of the former size should alone be used for the purpose under consideration. Such are decidedly cheaper in first cost per square foot of filtering surface; are as readily handled and kept tight, and require, proportionately to the work done, fewer laborers. They occupy scarcely more space.

The presses should be worked in batteries after the English plan, instead of by rotation, as practiced in Germany. This avoids a fall of pressure, with consequent loss of time and a cake ill suited to lixiviation in the other active presses, when one freshly prepared is set in operation. It also permits, which is of much consequence, low pressures at the start, which are gradually increased to high at the finish—a practice precluding all attempt at governing the pressure at the pump's throttle by an attached pressure regulator.

A precipitate invariably following evaporation, by whatever means accomplished, of juice filtered through brown coal, the filtration of sirup was accorded some study. For this purpose from 12 to 15 per cent. of lignite on the weight of sugar operated upon was found necessary to satisfactorily rapid work, previous treatment notwithstanding. Again the improvement in purity was not marked, averaging 0.82; that in color being the more conspicuous result, at about 40 per cent. of this removed.

For sirups from unfiltered juices the ratio of lignite had, of course, to be increased until percentages approaching those employed with juice had been attained. Equal amounts would probably have been necessary, in terms of sugar, except for scums removed and some 8 to 10 per cent. of the juice itself already filtered with these, decantation of clear liquor from skimmings not having been practiced. Mere bulk, thus, in the filtrate, was seen to exercise no perceptible influence in this work. The dilution of sirup by the addition of water in any amount can, of course, in no wise reduce the quantity of coal required, which is determined alone by the quantity and quality of non-sugar dealt with. Neither the net result in purity nor in color was equivalent in filtered sirup from unfiltered juice to that secured in unfiltered sirups from filtered juice. The glucose ratios of sirups first filtered as such were always considerably higher than those of unfiltered sirups derived from filtered juices of like quality. It is supposed that by the filtration of juice—though this is left in all cases more acid by the process—certain active inverting agents are removed, thus reducing the losses otherwise sustained in concentration. The brown coal also removed an amount of reducing sugars relatively larger than that of sucrose lost in the operation, the glucose ratio being almost uniformly lower after than before filtration, whether of juice or sirup. The ash is also reduced.

Not above 550 gallons of sirup from unfiltered juice could be put through a 30-frame Kroog press with 25 per cent. of brown coal on the weight of its sucrose at one operation, this, complete, occupying about four hours. A $\frac{7}{8}$-inch frame or chamber was found ample in the treatment of sirups, but even for this work 400-foot presses, it is thought, would be preferred. Thinner frames would be necessary with reduced percentages of lignite. Lower pressures than those mentioned for juice gave the more satisfactory results, which, also, should be extremely steady.

The cake from sirup filtrations following that of the juice, with or without lixiviation, when mixed with the amount of fresh coal necessary to bring the total of this to the usual standard, was found to perform about as well on a fresh supply of juice as an equal total of fresh coal; the amount of the latter being thus proportionately reduced. In practice this would obviate the difficulty of sweet water from the sirup filters. Wood char was given no trial in connection with concentrated liquors. The whole subject of sirup filtration, in filter presses, merits more thorough investigation than circumstances have yet permitted at this factory, although success with such can scarcely supplant the far greater necessity for previous treatment of the juices.

Experiments, by no means exhaustive, were also made with the Bauer process. This failed from the first. The mucilaginous impurities, passing through the interstices of the bone-char, reached and occluded at once the pores of the cloth, thus bringing operations to a speedy termination with every trial. The cloths were washed with great difficulty. To fully meet every prejudice, the entirely inutile use of various fabrics was resorted to. With bone-black, from coarse to finest, the result was always the same. Indeed, as is well known, animal char in sugar work is an extremely poor filtering medium, no matter how skillfully revivified, and except for the preliminary Taylor or bag filtration could scarcely be used after the manner or in the per cents. at present common, except upon the highest centrifugal goods, even in the refining of sugars from which the major portion of non-sugar has already been removed, upon the plantation, in scums, sediments, and molasses—substances which are yet left remaining with us in our treatment of juices. It is imperative with this article, in our work at least, that it be used in quantities quite beyond the utmost ability of filter-presses to accommodate.

Notwithstanding the meager results as yet secured, eventual success in the economic mechanical filtration of the entire body of defecated juice is not altogether despaired of. Its difficulties have been greatly underrated. All the juices thus far dealt with have been the product of milling under pressures attaining from 65 to 78 per cent.

of these upon the weight of canes crushed. So successful throughout
has been the routine work in this establishment with skimmings and
settlings from all manner of canes and with many modes of defecation, and so small has been at any time the immediate improvement
in the purity co-efficient attributable to it, and yet, by comparison,
so easy and rapid a second filtration, as to have forced a conviction
that in but an exceedingly small part of the total non-sugar resides
well nigh the whole difficulty. This probably minute portion of especially refractory material has been traced, as an insoluble, suspended
impurity, to raw juice direct from the rolls, which presents in the filter
practically all the perplexities encountered after defecation, and may
be followed thence quite to the molasses. The microscope has not
identified it at 100 diameters. Fermentation fails to remove it. Although itself probably inert and harmless, it suffices to render most difficult or altogether impossible a process which, in effecting an immediate
improvement, if only of several points in the exponent, would yet suffice
before the by-product was reached to add directly or indirectly a decided increment to the otherwise possible *rendement.* Your success in
filter-pressing carbonated diffusion juices this season of 1887–'88, at the
Magnolia Station, leads to the hope that this small part, whatever it
may be, is either in great measure eliminated from the artificial juice
by diffusion, or else is amenable to chemical treatment (other than
carbonation), such as it is reasonable to suppose will not escape adequate research. In either case the benefit to accrue would become important to the local industry, the substitution of osmosis for pressure in
juice extraction by large central factories now seeming as if eventually
inevitable.

It is proposed by the proprietor that the investigation of this subject
shall continue at this place uninterruptedly throughout another season.
At his desire I express the hope that it may not be impossible with
you to detail a chemist from your department to aid in this search for
an improved defecation. It is not to be overlooked how, to the present,
your department, in pursuing its inquiries with respect of sugar manufacture, has neglected altogether the sulphur regimen universally
found in Louisiana's practice, excepting only at its previou y chosen
station.

With much respect, sir, I am yours, very truly,
W. J. THOMPSON.

Dr. H. W. WILEY,
Chemist, U. S. Department of Agriculture,
Washington, D. O.

ILLUSTRATIONS.

15449—No. 17——8

CUTTER.

CUTTER

THE BATTERY.

DIRECTLY UNDER BATTERY.

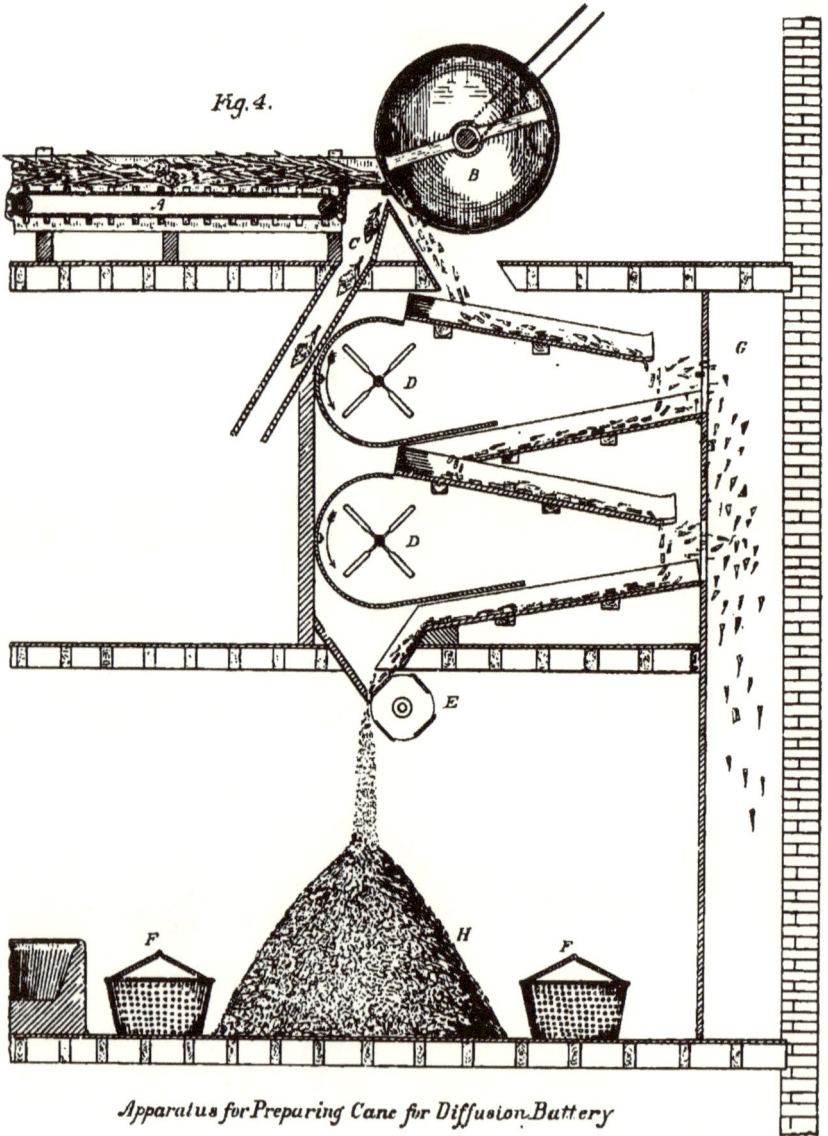

Fig. 4.

Apparatus for Preparing Cane for Diffusion Battery

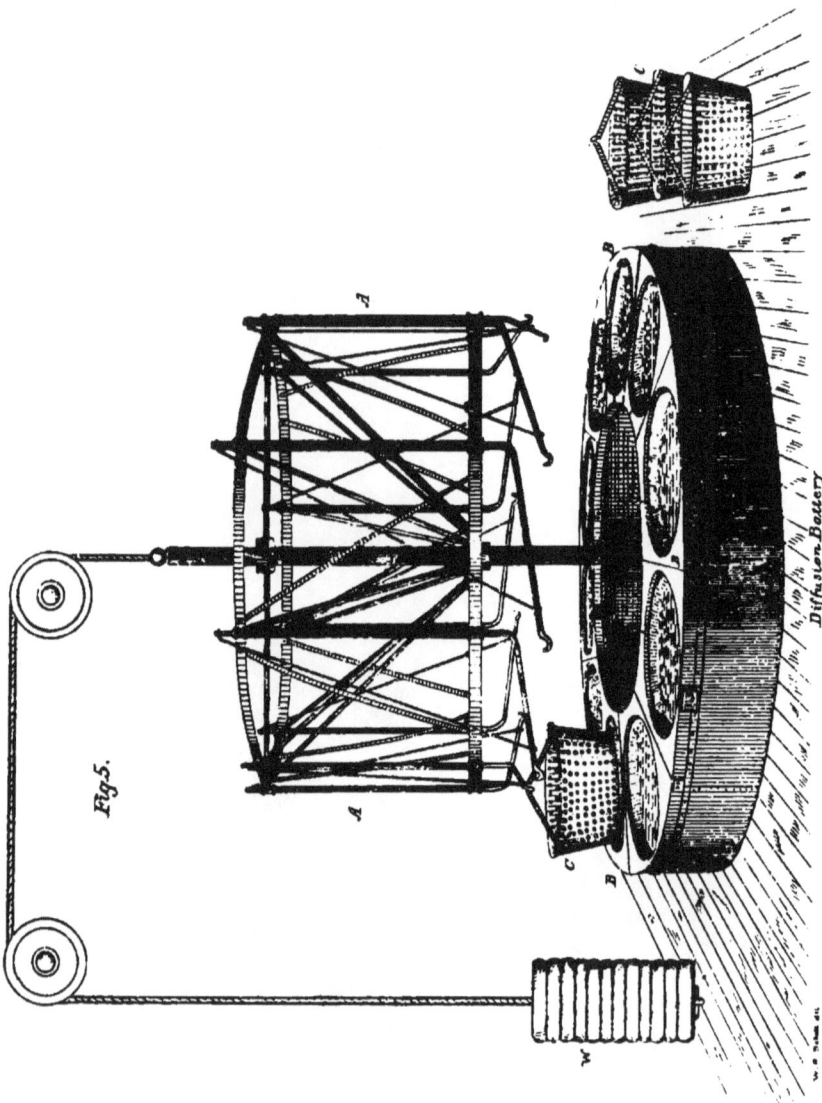

Fig.5.

Diffusion-Battery.

INDEX.

A.

B.

C.

D.

116

M.

T.

W.

Y.

○